Where Your Tax D

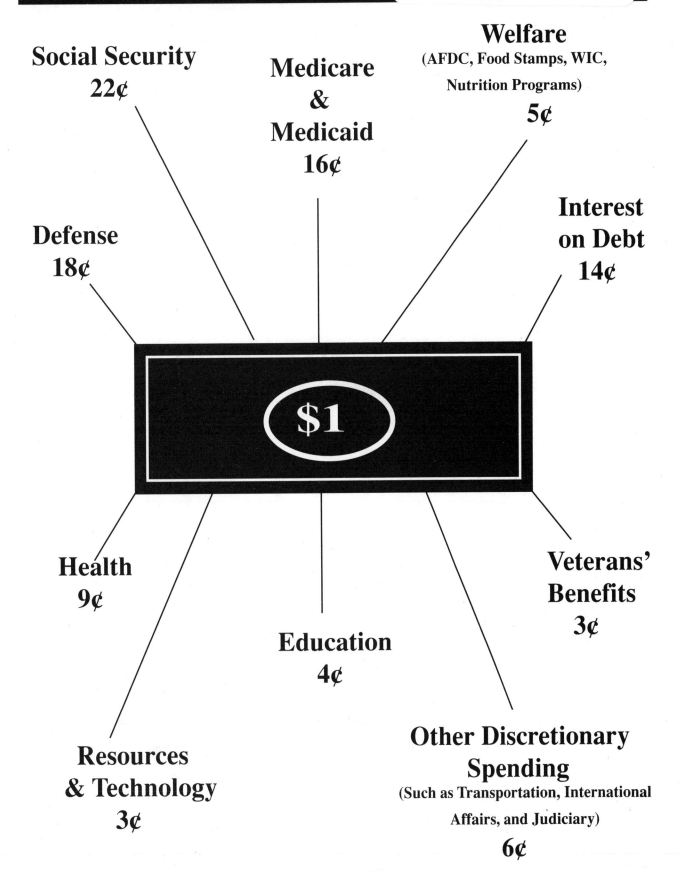

Social Security
22¢

Medicare
&
Medicaid
16¢

Welfare
(AFDC, Food Stamps, WIC,
Nutrition Programs)
5¢

Defense
18¢

Interest
on Debt
14¢

$1

Health
9¢

Veterans'
Benefits
3¢

Education
4¢

Resources
& Technology
3¢

Other Discretionary
Spending
(Such as Transportation, International
Affairs, and Judiciary)
6¢

How Much You Have Paid.....

The average taxpayer working for 30 years and earning about $30,000 per year (in real 1995 dollars) will have paid about $405,000 to the federal government, mainly due to the following programs:

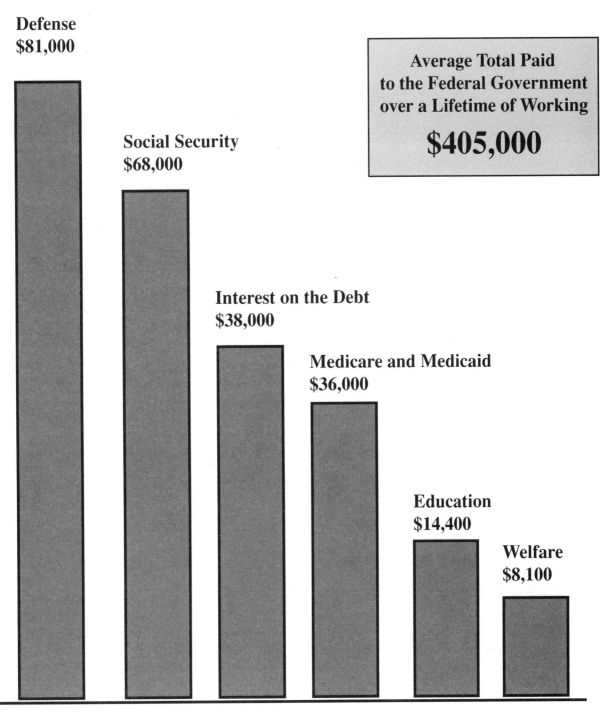

Defense
$81,000

Social Security
$68,000

Interest on the Debt
$38,000

Medicare and Medicaid
$36,000

Education
$14,400

Welfare
$8,100

**Average Total Paid
to the Federal Government
over a Lifetime of Working**

$405,000

Numbers calculated using U.S. Budgets 1965-1995 (from CBO and National Council of Economic Advisors) and federal tax rates for "single-filers" earning $30,000 in constant 1995 dollars (from IRS).

ANNUAL REPORT
OF THE
UNITED STATES
OF AMERICA

═══ 1996 ═══

ANNUAL REPORT
OF THE
UNITED STATES
OF AMERICA

═══ 1996 ═══

> **FEATURING A QUICK GUIDE TO THE**
> **1996 PRESIDENTIAL ELECTIONS**

What Every Citizen Should Know About
Where Each Tax Dollar
Goes and Why

MEREDITH E. BAGBY

HarperBusiness
A Division of HarperCollinsPublishers

Every effort has been made by the author to provide completely accurate and timely data and any changes in the information herein occurred after the information in this publication was gathered and printed.

HarperCollins books may be purchased for educational, business, or sales promotional use. For information please write: Special Markets Department, HarperCollins Publishers, Inc., 10 East 53rd Street, New York, NY 10022.

ISBN 0-88730-780-9

96 97 98 99 00 ❖ / CW 10 9 8 7 6 5 4 3 2 1

Contents

Special Thanks

*My greatest appreciation to **Ross Perot** for inspiring America and me to seek accountability from government and for taking my Annual Report before the U.S. Congress.*

*I would like to thank my parents, **Joseph and Martha Bagby**, and my grandmother, **Louise Green**, for their support, encouragement, and assistance in helping me produce this report. Many thanks to **Beth MacFall** for her constant help in production, to **Bonnie Cazin** for her research, and to **Chrissy DeNitto** and **Claire Johnson** for their continued contributions to this work.*

*Much appreciation to **Doe Coover**, my agent, and to **Adrian Zackheim** at HarperCollins for believing in the content.*

*Special acknowledgments go to **Dr. Dan Feenberg** of the National Bureau of Economic Research for his guidance in the art of research and to **Dr. Martin Feldstein,** Harvard professor of economics and president of the National Bureau of Economic Research, for inspiring me in economics.*

*At HarperCollins I would like to recognize my editor, **Kirsten Sandberg**, for her constant care in preparing this report; **Lisa Berkowitz, Breene Farrington,** and **Maureen O'Neill** for their publicity efforts; and to **Ashok Chaudhari, C. Linda Dingler, Kim Lewis,** and **Susan Kosko**, for their editorial and production support.*

I thank the many people who continue to write to me offering their endorsements and comments. These suggestions make this second report stronger. I always need your advice to make this publication better in future editions. Please continue to send your letters to:

HarperBusiness
A Division of HarperCollins Publishers
10 East 53rd Street
New York, NY 10022-5299

Attn: Meredith E. Bagby
Annual Report of the U.S.A.

Reclaiming Our Power

A Letter to My Fellow Americans

Dear Citizens:

America is truly at a watershed in its history. American citizens and voters have grown dissatisfied with the political leadership of our country and the downsizing of our standard of living.

Politically we have become disgusted with the gridlock in Washington. Our politicians seem to fight one another more than solve America's problems. This frustration with partisan politics and the desire for change are what ultimately called our attention to an unknown governor from Arkansas, propelled the support for the Contract with America, and established the first Republican majority in the Congress in forty years.

Dissatisfaction with the status quo fueled the following of Ross Perot when he ran as an independent candidate for president in 1992 and it now drives General Colin Powell's presidential appeal.

Our anger with the political system causes us to seek new candidates and institutions other than those offered by the two-party system. The Christian Coalition, the Libertarian Party, and the United We Stand America organization led by Ross Perot draw the support of Americans who feel ostracized and ignored by the current political system.

Frustrated by Bureaucracy

Hand-in-hand with our disenchantment with the political process is our skepticism of bureaucracy. We are desperately rethinking our conception of government. Historically, two visions of government have battled in the United States. The first, associated today with the Democratic Party, is a government of strong national power in which states' and local rights are subordinate to the federal government. This government promises a greater degree of economic equality through federally funded programs. It also imposes more restrictions on private institutions in order to maintain (1) safety and security and (2) fairness and equal rights.

A second vision of government, traditionally associated with the Republican Party, focuses instead on limiting the scope of federal government and giving greater responsibility to the individual. This government is less likely (1) to impose restrictions on private institutions and (2) to redistribute wealth in society but more likely to invest power in states and localities to deal with the problems in their midst such as poverty and education.

Throughout our history these two concepts of government have balanced national interests with state interests, capitalism with responsibility, freedom with equality. We see in our government today that the latter vision, the concept of the Republicans, has become a powerful, dynamic force in shaping our public policy.

The American people show despondency about many of the social trends in our nation. One trend is the breakup of the family. Since the 1950s Americans have been moving away from the traditional nuclear family, in which mom stays home and dad works. For many this move causes concern; they argue that the splitting of the family is producing children who gravitate more toward drugs, crime, and suicide.

Many contend that these trends generate a permanent underclass. Today nearly 30 percent of all children are born into single-parent families usually headed by women and are four times more likely to find themselves in poverty. Forty percent of all those in poverty are children. Many urge the government to do more to keep families together and to teach ethics and values in school. The Christian Coalition, for instance, published the Contract with the American Family. They and many more will take their message to the polls when electing a president in 1996.

Americans feel increasing resentment about the rise in crime, drugs, suicide, and homelessness in our cities and the spread of all of these into our suburbs. There is a call to answer concerns of racial inequality. There are concerns about the question of affirmative action.

Internationally, America struggles to redefine itself in a post–cold war world. Ethnic tension and nationalism continue to emerge around the globe, causing disturbances in Eastern Europe, Africa, and the Middle East.

The United States must learn how to lead and manuever in a new and complex world. With domestic issues becoming our primary concerns, we struggle to maintain our foreign agendas. In forming policy we must answer fundamental questions. What role does America want to play in world politics? What resources is America willing to commit to our foreign policy?

With America more dependent on foreign trade, we must keep good relations in Europe and North America while developing new ties with China, Kenya, India, Argentina, and Brazil. We must also remember that our military and economic policies are linked throughout the world and require balance.

Can America continue to exist as one nation with so many factions now tearing at us? One study by *Newsweek* reports that nearly 50 percent of Americans do not even believe that America will exist as one nation 100 years from today. This study calls into debate our basic tenets as a society. Indeed, what keeps us together as a nation? What does it mean to be an American, and what does America want from a world that awaits it?

Despite reports of apathy, America has, perhaps, the most interactive and vital electorate in the world. For this reason we can devise solutions for our future.

This, my *Second Annual Report of the United States of America*, is organized to present to you a wide look at the mainstreams that are forging our nation anew. To understand where we are today as a nation, we present:

(1) The Social State of the Nation, which provides you with a glance at the major social trends facing America—from Medicare reform to crime to abortion to Social Security.

(2) The Political State of the Nation, which reviews the Republican and Democratic parties' promises and results. You can also compare the presidential candidates for 1996 and their platforms.

(3) The Economic State of the Nation, which shows us how we are performing financially by discussing the major economic indicators of our economic growth.

(4) The International State of the Nation, which explores our military strategy, foreign policy, international trade, and the environment.

(5) The Financial Review, which provides the financial statements of our federal government.

America belongs to us as citizens and as shareholders. The more we understand as involved stockholders, the more exciting and productive America can be. This is why I offer you this report for the second year.

I thank all of you who have sent letters and suggestions to me about my first report. I hope that you will find this report informative, stimulating, and useful as a basis to understand more about how our government is using our tax dollars. I need your continued comments so that next year's report can be even more inclusive of the facts you want to know as Americans.

Sincerely,

Meredith Bagby

Meredith E. Bagby

Who We Are

Our Population

The United States of America is a nation of 263 million in a world of 5.7 billion people. We consist of 50 states and the District of Columbia, American Samoa, Baker Island and Jarvis Island, Guam, Howland Island, Johnston Island and Sand Island, Kingman Reef, Midway Island, Northern Mariana Islands, Palmyra Island, Puerto Rico, Trust Territory of the Pacific Island, Virgin Islands of the U.S., and Wake Island.

Ethnicity

The majority of Americans, about 73 percent, are of European descent. The majority of those claim ancestry of German (23.3 percent), Irish (15.6 percent), or English (13.1 percent). The largest minority remains African-American, but within the next 15 years Hispanics will likely become the number one minority.

Language

More than 31 million of us speak a language other than English at home; more than half this number speak Spanish. In 1990, four in ten New Yorkers over the age of five spoke a foreign language at home.

Religion

Most Americans identify themselves as Christians. The largest non-Christian religion is Judaism.

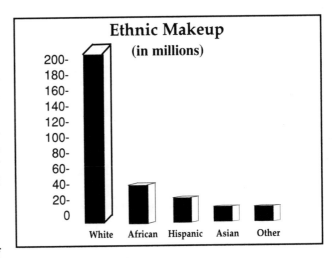

Age

We are an aging population. Since 1980, our median age has risen from 30.0 to 34.0 in 1994, because of the aging of the baby boomers and our increased life span. The fastest-growing group in America is 85-year-olds and over.

Residence

At least half of our population (56.4 percent) lives in the South and West regions of the country. In the 1980s and 1990s, more than half the country's population growth was concentrated in California, Florida, and Texas. More than half our people, about 130 million Americans, live in a metropolitan area of more than 1 million.

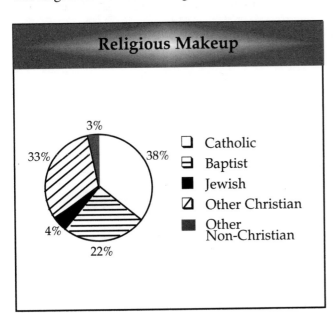

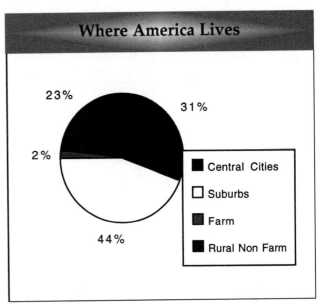

Our Economy

Makeup of Economy

A major portion of our economy is devoted to the production of petroleum, fertilizer, cement, pig iron, plastics, newsprint, natural gas, and electricity. The U.S. is also known for its high export sales in machinery, chemicals, motor vehicles, aircrafts, military equipment, and grains.

Our Changing Economy

Over the past decade, our economy has become more diverse and complex.

First, our economy has grown increasingly dependent on foreign trade. Nearly 40 percent of all our economic growth last year was in exports. In addition 30 percent of our entire economy is based in trade.

Another highly important development is the new emphasis on education. The blue-collar jobs that once kept overall incomes rising have either moved abroad or disappeared because of technology.

New jobs created in America will now be in the service industry and in high technology. We see that since 1960, the growth in service jobs has been on the rise while there has been little to no growth in manufacturing.

Growth

The growth in our economy as measured by the change in Gross Domestic Product (GDP) is presently around 2.5 percent (real rate), a decrease from a 1994 fourth quarter high of 5.1 percent. GDP is a measure of how much is produced in the U.S. in a given year.

Many economists argue that our economy is now

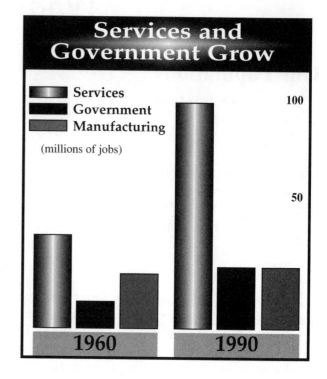

working at full capacity—that is, we have decreased unemployment as much as we can (without increasing inflation).

While our growth rates are not so high as those experienced after World War II, they do ensure steady growth and rising incomes in the future. Economists tend to agree that we can only increase this growth rate long term through increased investment and savings.

Measures of Economic Health

Our unemployment rate remains steady at 5.7 percent after a small rise in March 1995. Inflation remains about 3 percent. Retail sales this year are up 3.2 percent, barely outpacing inflation.

This past year, the U.S. dollar's value fell in comparison to most of the industrialized countries. The devaluation follows the Mexican peso crisis. Exports are expected to grow by 12.5 percent this coming year.

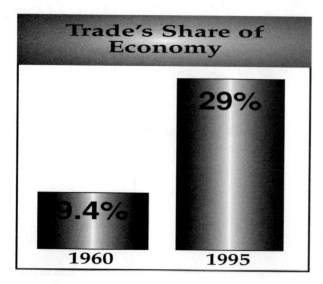

Basic Statistics	
Gross Domestic Product	$6,379.4 billion
Per Capita Personal Income	$20,817
Median Family Income	$32,264
Civilian Labor Force	130.7 million

Our Family

There are 96 million households in our nation; 70 percent of these are families. The average number of persons per household is 2.63.

Of all households, 55 percent are maintained by married couples. Two-parent families account for 36 percent of family households, down from 50 percent in 1970.

The number of never-married persons doubled from 21.4 million to 42.3 million from 1970 to present. The number of unmarried-couples households is 3.5 million, seven times larger than in 1970.

Mom

Mom is spending more time working and less time with her children and her husband than her mother did. Still, she spends about 45 hours a week with her family, compared with 36 hours working.

Mom is also more likely to raise a child alone. Nearly 30 percent of all family groups with children are maintained by single parents (usually mothers), a significant increase from 12 percent in 1970.

Dad

Dad spends more time at work than mom and less time with his children. He works an average of 62 hours a week and spends 20 hours a week with his children.

Dad is also less likely to remain with his family. More families are now headed by single mothers, particularly in the African-American community. Nearly 70 percent of all black children are born out of wedlock. Statistics show that a father is less likely to remain an active part of his children's lives if he is not marrried to their mother.

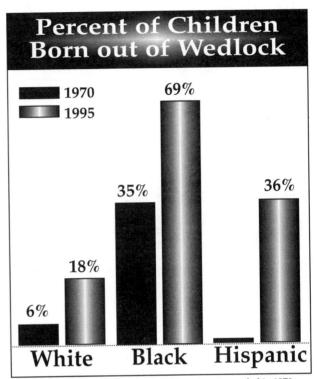

Source: Current population survey. *Hispanic not recorded in 1970.

There is also evidence that many men do not pay adequate support for the children they father. From all those owed child support from a father, about half receive the full amount they are due. The average amount of child support received in 1989 was $2,995. The aggregate amount of child support received in 1989 was $11.2 billion–69 percent of $16.3 billion due.

Children

A growing number of children live in single-parent families or with extended family (e.g., grandparents). These families are more likely to slip into poverty. Now, children under the age of 18 account for 40 percent of the poor.

The annual cost of child care services is roughly $3,500 per child. Poor families spend over 20 percent of their monthly income on child care compared to about 7 percent for families above the poverty line.

Most care for pre-schoolers takes place in a home environment, with relatives or neighbors (67 percent); about 23 percent of child care for pre-schoolers is in organized facilities, such as nursery and day-care centers; 9 percent are cared for by the mother while she works; and 1 percent are in a school-based activity.

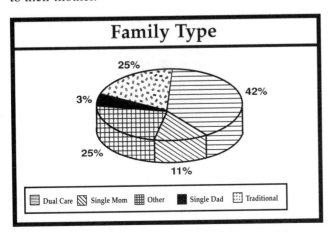

Our Income

The Labor Force

About 66 percent of Americans 16 years and older are in the labor force–almost 76 percent of men and 58 percent of women. The number of women in the labor force has been steadily growing since 1960.

Our top three occupations are administrative support, professional specialty and executive, and managerial. There are 20.2 million persons employed in the retail sales industry, almost 10 percent of our population.

Income Growth

While our economy has been growing, our incomes have not maintained the levels of the late 1980s. In 1995, our median family income is $32,254, below the 1989 high of $34,445. However, our wages did grow from 1993 to 1994. Many attribute this increase in wages, at least in part, to an increase in hours worked, particularly by women in families.

Income Distribution

The number of Americans living below the poverty line has decreased for the first time since 1989. In 1994 those below the poverty line decreased by 1.2 million, giving us a poverty rate of 14.5 percent.

The gap between income groups continued to rise

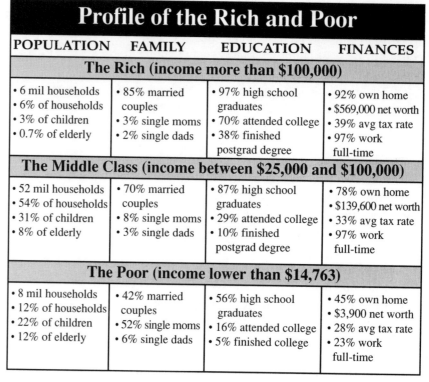

POPULATION	FAMILY	EDUCATION	FINANCES
The Rich (income more than $100,000)			
• 6 mil households • 6% of households • 3% of children • 0.7% of elderly	• 85% married couples • 3% single moms • 2% single dads	• 97% high school graduates • 70% attended college • 38% finished postgrad degree	• 92% own home • $569,000 net worth • 39% avg tax rate • 97% work full-time
The Middle Class (income between $25,000 and $100,000)			
• 52 mil households • 54% of households • 31% of children • 8% of elderly	• 70% married couples • 8% single moms • 3% single dads	• 87% high school graduates • 29% attended college • 10% finished postgrad degree	• 78% own home • $139,600 net worth • 33% avg tax rate • 97% work full-time
The Poor (income lower than $14,763)			
• 8 mil households • 12% of households • 22% of children • 12% of elderly	• 42% married couples • 52% single moms • 6% single dads	• 56% high school graduates • 16% attended college • 5% finished college	• 45% own home • $3,900 net worth • 28% avg tax rate • 23% work full-time

Profile of the Rich and Poor

with the top 20 percent of the income distribution earning 49.1 percent of all income and the bottom 20 percent earning just 3.6 percent.

Income groups do have particular characteristics. The most notable difference is educational achievement. Seventy percent of the rich attended college compared to 16 percent of the poor. While inequality among income groups is on the rise, inequality among the races and the sexes is decreasing. Black households were the only group to show a significant increase in median income last year. In addition, women's and men's incomes are growing closer—although they are still far from equal. A woman makes about 70 cents for every dollar a man earns.

Female to Male (full-time workers) $.70 to $1.00

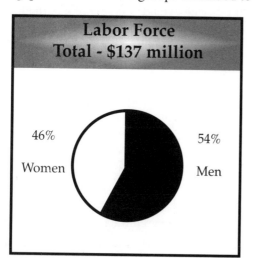

Labor Force Total - $137 million

46% Women

54% Men

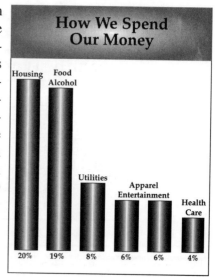

How We Spend Our Money

Housing 20% | Food Alcohol 19% | Utilities 8% | Apparel Entertainment 6% | Entertainment 6% | Health Care 4%

Financial Highlights

The United States Budget

Net Income

The money that the government collects. Most of this money comes from taxes, of which there are many kinds.

(millions of dollars)	(actual)		(estimates*)		
	1993	1994	1995	1996	1997
Individual Income Taxes	$509,700	$549,901	$595,048	$627,700	$664,100
Corporation Income Taxes	117,520	130,719	104,437	145,000	149,800
Excise Taxes	48,057	54,600	71,888	71,700	72,700
Social Insurance Taxes	428,300	461,923	490,393	518,300	548,500
Custom Duties	18,802	19,198	20,856	21,300	22,200
Estate and Gift Taxes	12,577	12,749	13,885	15,000	16,100
All Other Miscellaneous	18,579	19,981	57,308	28,300	31,700
NET INCOME	$1,153,535	$1,249,071	$1,353,815	$1,427,300	$1,505,100

* Based on U.S. 1995 budget.

Individual Income Tax

A tax levied on your salary and any other income you have, for instance, in the stock market or from your savings account. A progressive tax.

Corporate Income Tax

A tax levied as a percentatge of corporate income. A progressive tax.

Excise Taxes

A tax levied on certain commodities like tobacco or alcohol. Excise taxes tend to be popular politically. For instance, many suggest that we tax cigarettes so that we encourage people to smoke less. We also put excise taxes on oil so that people will consume less gas.

Customs Duties

Taxes put on food and goods coming into the U.S. For instance, the tax on Japanese cars.

Social Insurance Tax

A tax taken out of wages before the salary ever reaches the individual. The money then put in a fund goes to pay for the Social Security benefits of the elderly, retired, and disabled. The tax exists to ensure that people will have something to live on once they become too old to work.

Estate and Gift Taxes

Estate taxes are put on personal property at the time of death. Gift taxes are levied on large gifts given from one person to another.

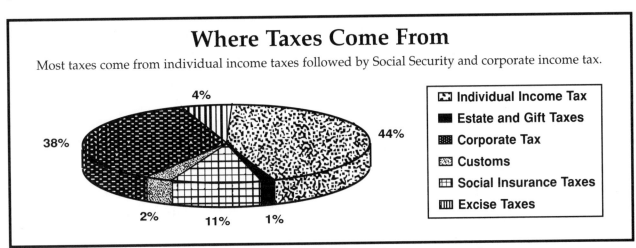

Where Taxes Come From

Most taxes come from individual income taxes followed by Social Security and corporate income tax.

4%
38%
44%
2%   11%   1%

- Individual Income Tax
- Estate and Gift Taxes
- Corporate Tax
- Customs
- Social Insurance Taxes
- Excise Taxes

Net Expenses

Anything that the government spends. Includes everything from the cost of building roads to the president's salary to grants to research and development. The government spends our money in essentially two ways: transfer payments and service payments.

(millions of dollars)	(actual) 1993	1994	(estimate*) 1995	1996	1997
Service Payments					
International Affairs	$16,826	$18,968	$17,798	$17,900	$17,700
Judiciary	$14,955	$16,479	$17,331	$19,600	$21,000
Science/Technology	$17,030	$17,279	$16,941	$16,700	$16,700
Transportation	$35,004	$37,582	$38,368	$20,400	$20,400
Natural Resources	$20,239	$22,285	$21,817	$22,100	$22,100
Defense	$291,086	$279,824	$270,725	$261,000	$256,400
Education	$50,012	$50,793	$53,524	$54,200	$55,420
Energy	$4,319	$4,988	$4,564	$4,700	$4,800
Health	$99,415	$112,252	$123,077	$149,600	$180,000
Community Development	$9,051	$9,282	$9,154	$8,900	$8,500
Transfer Payments					
Social Security	$304,585	$320,460	$337,168	$356,800	$374,700
Housing Credit	-$22,725	-$504	-$5,482	-$9,000	-$5,700
Medicare	$130,552	$143,651	$156,228	$176,000	$195,800
Income Security	$207,257	$214,626	$221,440	$230,000	$242,500
Veterans' Benefits	$35,720	$38,129	$39,247	$38,200	$41,500
Interest on the Public Debt	$198,811	$203,448	$212,835	$224,200	$234,000
Other Miscellaneous Exp.	($3,932)	($5,713)	($15,790)	($5,800)	($5,580)
Net Expenses	**$1,408,205**	**$1,483,829**	**$1,518,945**	**$1,596,900**	**$1,691,400**
DEFICIT	**$254,670**	**$234,758**	**$165,130**	**$169,600**	**$186,300**

* Based on U.S. budget 1995.

Transfer Payments

Transfer payments occur when the government transfers money from one group in society to another, for example, when the government taxes the general public in order to give money to the poor in the form of welfare or when the government distributes money to the elderly in the form of Social Security.

Some other transfer payments are the Commerce and Housing Credit, which gives money to people who cannot provide housing for themselves. Another example is Medicare, which provides health care for the elderly.

Service Payments

Service payments occur when the government buys a particular service for the U.S. Examples include building roads, providing for our national defense, or investing in science by financing a space shuttle.

Net Interest

Net interest is the amount we pay each year on our debt. In simple terms, it is this amount that the government has to pay for taking out loans.

Government pays interest by meeting its obligations on U.S. bonds or bills sold to investors. Each year that amount gets larger because each year the U.S. accumulates more debt.

Deficit

This is income minus expenses, or the amount the federal government takes in from taxes, subtracting the amount that the federal goverment spends. For the last 25 years this number has been negative. The new congressional budget bill for fiscal year 1996 seeks to end the deficit and balance the budget within the next seven years.

Understanding the Debt

Deficit

The difference between what the government receives in taxes and what it pays out for various government services is the deficit. Throughout the 1980s, the U.S. began running large deficits when President Reagan initiated large tax cuts but was unable to pass

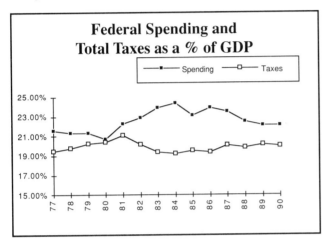

Federal Spending and Total Taxes as a % of GDP

spending cuts through Congress. The graph shows the wedge between income and expenses in the United States. To finance the deficit, the government has borrowed money from its citizens and from foreign investors. This borrowing transformed America from the largest creditor nation in the world to the largest debtor nation.

The graph above shows the deficit over a period of years. Both the president and Congress are now making attempts to balance the budget and reduce the deficit. If no drastic changes are made, the projected deficit into the '90s will hover around $200 billion.

Interest on the Debt

The third largest expense for our federal government is paying the interest on our debt. In 1995, the United States paid almost $220 billion of interest just on the debt. Because our debt is projected to grow, the interest on the debt will continue to rise, perhaps becoming our largest single expense. The interest on the debt is the financing cost of debt, the interest we pay to people, corporations, and institutions holding government securities.

The Debt

The U.S. debt is the money that the government borrows, usually to finance the accumulation of the deficit. The debt is the amount that the government owes

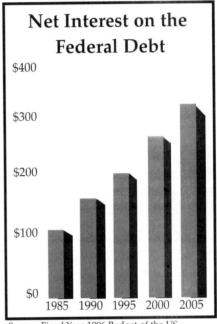

Net Interest on the Federal Debt

Source: Fiscal Year 1996 Budget of the US Governement CBO 1995

either to its people or to institutions or to foreign countries that invest in U.S. securities.

The U.S. debt is presently close to $5 trillon and projected to grow into the year 2000.

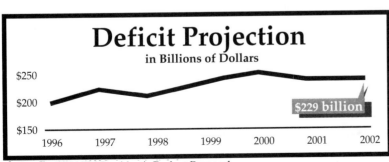

Deficit Projection
in Billions of Dollars

$229 billion

Source: FY 1996 President's Budget Proposal

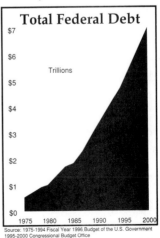

Total Federal Debt

Trillions

Source: 1975-1994 Fiscal Year 1996 Budget of the U.S. Government
1995-2000 Congressional Budget Office

America's Net Worth

In order to calculate the "net worth" of a company, liabilities are subtracted from assets. As you can imagine, it is very complicated to put together a balance sheet and calculate a net worth for the U.S. government.

The Treasury Department, though, has made an attempt to put together such a balance sheet. Perhaps the best reporting done was a report put together by Arthur Andersen & Co. under the direction of the Treasury Department.

The following information and charts come from this 1993 report. Excerpts from this report are in the *Financial Review,* with a complete set of financial statements.

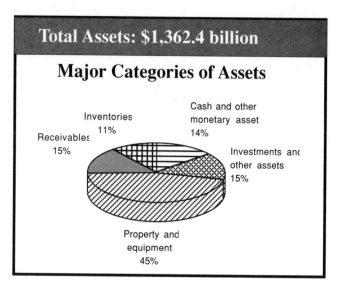

Assets

The 1993 report attempts to calculate the total assets of the federal government. As the graph shows, the government's main assets are property and equipment, cash, investments, and inventories. In total the federal government has $1.36 trillion in assets.

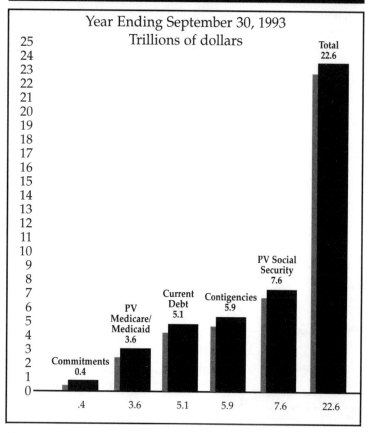

Liabilities

Liabilities of the federal government were estimated to be $5,239 billion. These liabilities include the debt held as U.S. Securities, pension, and actuarial liabilities as well as other monies owed. For a complete breakdown, see the *Financial Review.*

Net Worth

According to the 1993 report, the net worth of the U.S. government is a negative $3,876 billion. In other words, if you sold off all assets of the federal government, it would not be able to pay its current obligations; it would still owe $3,876,600,000 (just under $4 billion).

Future Obligations

The chart to the left details the future obligations of the federal government, totaling $22.8 trillion. The total obligations of the federal government are about $85,000 for every man, woman, and child in the U.S.

Liabilities include: (1) $7.6 trillion, which represents the present value of Social Security payments, (2) $5.9 trillion in contingent liabilities such as rents on land, obligations to RTC and other independent agencies, (3) $5.1 trillion in debt held as U.S. securities, (4) $3.6 trillion representing the present value of Medicare and Medicaid obligations, and (5) $.4 trillion in commitments or monies owed for various services rendered.

Focus on the Budget

The Budget Debate

Facts About the Budget

The government spends most of your money on a few major programs. In 1995, Defense, Social Security, Medicare, Medicaid, and interest payments on the national debt account for over 70 percent of all federal spending.

Other controversial programs such as Aid to Families with Dependent Children and foreign aid actually account for smaller portions of spending. Together, these two programs account for less than 3 percent of all federal spending.

Spending comes in two varieties–discretionary and mandatory:

Discretionary spending, which accounts for 36 percent of all federal spending, is the money the president and Congress must decide to spend each year for such programs as the FBI, the Coast Guard, housing, space exploration, highway constructions, defense, and foreign aid.

Mandatory spending, which accounts for 64 percent of all spending, is the money that the federal government spends automatically, on entitlements such as Social Security, Medicare, and food stamps, and on interest on the national debt.

Despite its name, mandatory spending is not fixed in stone. The president and Congress can vote to change the laws that govern entitlements.

Rise in Mandatory Spending

As a share of the budget, mandatory spending has soared in recent decades. The increase in mandatory spending is due to the rise in entitlement spending and in net interest on the national debt.

1. Perhaps the most popular federal program ever, Social Security, provides monthly benefits to over 43 million retired and disabled workers, their dependents and survivors. The program has expanded steadily since its creation in the 1930s. Today, it accounts for 22 percent of all federal spending.

2. Medicare, which provides health care coverage for over 37 million elderly Americans, includes Part A, hospital insurance, and Part B, insurance for physicians and other services. Since its birth in 1965, it has accounted for a larger and larger share of spending. Today, it measures 10 percent.

3. Medicaid, the health care program for the poor, also was established in 1965. Unlike Medicare, however, the federal government shares costs with the states. Medicaid, which provides services to over 36 million Americans, accounts for 6 percent of the budget.

4. The costs of Aid to Families with Dependent Children (AFDC), the main federal welfare program, are shared with the states. AFDC, established in 1935, provides cash and services to needy children and their families and accounts for 1 percent of federal spending.

5. Net interest payments on the debt consumed only about 7 percent of federal spending for most of the 1960s and 1970s. With the huge deficits in recent years, that share quickly doubled to 14 percent today.

Three Plans for Reform

On a mission to balance the budget, the House, the Senate, and the president have all been struggling to bring the U.S. budget into balance. Because citizens have shown support for spending cuts rather than tax increases, the government has proposed to decrease spending and even decrease tax rates.

The House's original plan for the budget was very similar to the plan written about in the Contract with America. The budget resolution called for spending cuts to balance the budget by 2002 along with tax cuts totaling $281 billion dollars over the next seven years.

The measure called for the reduction in the spending of nearly all federal programs, except the Defense Department, and had sizable cuts in Medicare and Medicaid.

The Senate passed a budget resolution which was somewhat more moderate than the House's. The Sen-

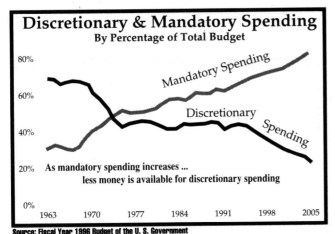

Discretionary & Mandatory Spending
By Percentage of Total Budget

Mandatory Spending

Discretionary Spending

As mandatory spending increases ...
less money is available for discretionary spending

80%
60%
40%
20%
0%
1963   1970   1977   1984   1991   1998   2005

Source: Fiscal Year 1996 Budget of the U. S. Government

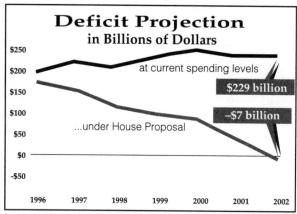

Deficit Projection
in Billions of Dollars

at current spending levels

$229 billion

–$7 billion

...under House Proposal

Source: Fiscal Year 1996 Budget of the U. S. Government

ate called for fewer tax cuts. In addition, the Senate delayed those tax cuts until Congress passes legislation that balances the budget.

The Senate resolution also calls for smaller reductions in Medicare and Medicaid and allows for less spending in defense programs.

In contrast to these primarily Republican plans is President Clinton's bill, which would have balanced the budget in ten years rather than seven. President Clinton also proposed smaller tax cuts, targeted at taxpayers earning less than $100,000. His reductions in Medicare and Medicaid were smaller. In addition, Clinton's bill would have increased spending for education and training programs.

The Compromise

The agreement on the Congressional budget plan will be a Republican victory. It is still unclear, though, how the president will accept the bill. The new bill incorporates many of the ideas in the Contract with America and looks very similar to the House's original bill:

Balancing the Budget — The agreement calls for cutting the deficit by $40 billion in fiscal year 1996, and a total of $1.2 trillion over the next seven years.

Medicare — The agreement calls for major changes to the Medicare program in order to reduce spending by $270 billion over seven years ($18 billion less than the House resolution) compared to the spending levels required under current law.

Medicaid — Under the agreement, the growth in Medicaid funding would be limited to 4 percent per year by FY 1998, saving $182 billion through FY 2002, $5 billion less than in the House resolution.

Guaranteed Student Loans — The measure assumes a

$10 billion reduction in student loan programs.

Agriculture — The agreement assumes a $13.4 billion cut in farm programs, $3.6 billion less than the House bill.

Welfare Reform — The measure assumes the enactment of Republican welfare reform legislation and changes in the Earned Income Tax Credit (EITC) that would cut spending by $100 billion over seven years.

Discretionary Caps and "Firewalls" — The agreement sets discretionary budget and outlay caps below the fiscal year 1995 level in each of the next seven fiscal years and reinstates separate defense and nondefense spending caps for the next three fiscal years.

Tax Cuts — The agreement provides for reducing federal taxes by $245 billion over seven years, but prohibits Senate consideration of tax cuts until the Congressional Budget Office certifies that the spending cuts in the reconciliation bill will achieve a balanced budget by fiscal year 2002.

The Reaction

Republicans in the House and Senate are very pleased with the upcoming budget bill. Budget Committee chairman Pete Domenici of New Mexico, said the budget resolution was adopted in "the same revolutionary spirit of the Boston Tea Party."

With the same type of enthusiasm, Robert Walker, vice chairman of the House Budget Committee, said that the Republicans have succeeded in a way that no one thought they would. "We have proved the naysayers wrong. We have followed through on our promises."

In contrast, the Democrats are not pleased with the new budget resolution, saying that the plan gives benefits to the wealthy through tax breaks at the expense of the poor and elderly.

Senator Jim Exon of Nebraska, a ranking Democrat on the Budget Committee, said that the Republican budget "has no heart and lacks a soul."

CHANGES IN CURRENT SPENDING (In billions of dollars)

	1996	1997	1998	1999	2000	2001	2002	TOTAL
Defense	6	8	8	9	9	9	9	**58**
Nondefense	-10	-23	-27	-31	-31	-34	-35	**-190**
Social Security	-	-	-	-	-	-	-	
Medicare	-8	-18	-27	-37	-49	-60	-71	**-270**
Medicaid	-4	-8	-16	-24	-33	-43	-54	**-182**
Other mandatory	-10	-1	-25	-26	-29	-30	-36	**-182**
Revenue	-	-	-	-		-1	-1	**-3**
Debt service	1	-5	-9	-16	-24	-35	-48	**-137**
TOTAL DEFICIT REDUCTION	-28	-64	-95	125	-157	-193	-236	**$-898**

Source: U.S. Senate Budget Committee

Corporate Welfare

A study done this year by the Cato Institute shows that the federal budget contains more than 125 programs that subsidize private business, and in fiscal year 1995, more than $85 billion of the taxpayers' money will be spent on these programs. The following list includes some of the more egregious taxpayer subsidies to industries and firms.

• **Sematech:** A consortium of very large U.S. computer microchip producers receives from the Pentagon nearly $100 million a year of support. Of the more than 200 chipmakers in the United States, only the 14 largest, including Intel and National Semiconductor, receive federal support from Sematech.

• **Sugar Farms:** An estimated 40 percent of the $1.4 billion sugar price support program benefits the largest 1 percent of sugar farms. The 33 largest sugar cane plantations each receive more than $1 million per year.

• **Electric Utility:** Through the Rural Electrification Administration and the Federal Power Marketing Administrations, the federal government provides some $2 billion in subsidies each year to large and profitable electric utility cooperatives, such as ALLTEL, which had sales of $2.3 billion last year. Federally subsidized electricity holds down the costs of running ski resorts in Aspen, Colorado, five-star hotels in Hilton Head, South Carolina, and gambling casinos in Las Vegas, Nevada.

• **Forest Service:** Last year the Forest Service spent $140 million building roads in national forests, thus subsidizing the removal of timber from federal lands by multimillion-dollar timber companies. Over the past 20 years, the Forest Service has built 340,000 miles of roads–more than eight times the length of the interstate highway system–primarily for the benefit of logging companies.

• **Department of Agriculture:** The Department of Agriculture Market Promotion Program spends $110 million per year underwriting the cost of advertising American products abroad. In 1991, American taxpayers spent $2.9 million advertising Pillsbury muffins and pies, $10 million promoting Sunkist oranges, $465,000 advertising McDonald's Chicken McNuggets, $1.2 million boosting the international sales of American Legend mink coats, and

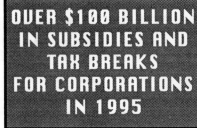

OVER $100 BILLION IN SUBSIDIES AND TAX BREAKS FOR CORPORATIONS IN 1995

$2.5 million extolling the virtues of Dole pineapples, nuts, and prunes.

• **Environmental Cleanup and Defense Contractors:** Last year a House of Representatives investigative team discovered that federal environmental cleanup and defense contractors had been milking federal taxpayers for millions of dollars in entertainment, recreation, and party expenses. Martin Marietta Corporation charged the Pentagon $263,000 for a Smokey Robinson concert, $20,000 for the purchase of golf balls, and $7,500 for a 1993 office Christmas party. Ecology and Environment, Inc., of Lancaster, New York, spent $243,000 of funds designated for environment cleanup on "employee morale" and $37,000 on tennis lessons, bike races, golf tournaments, and entertainment.

The Clinton Record

Much of the Clinton administration's interest in corporate grants and subsidies is in promoting what it refers to as "strategically important" high-technology products and research efforts. In this year's budget, the Clinton administration has requested the following:

• $490 million for the Advanced Technology Program. Last year the administration provided grant funds to such industry giants as General Electric, United Airlines, Xerox, Dupont, and Caterpillar.

• $500 million for the Technology Reinvestment Project, a newly created military defense conversion program that subsidizes the development of civilian technologies. In 1994 award recipients included such Fortune 500 companies as Texas Instruments, Inc. ($13 million), 3M Co. ($6 million), Chrysler Corporation ($6 million), Hewlett Packard ($10 million), Boeing Co. ($7 million), and Rockwell International Corp. ($7 million).

• $333 million for the New Generation of Vehicles program, of the "Clean Car Initiative," which the White House says will "ensure the global competitiveness of the U.S. automobile industry"—that is, GM, Ford, and Chrysler. In 1994, Detroit's Big Three had a record $13.9 billion in profits.

• $9.4 billion in Small Business Administration loan guarantees, an increase of nearly 50 percent since 1993.

• The Democratic Leadership Council's Progressive Policy Institute has specified some 30 such "tax subsidies" that led to a loss of $134 billion in federal revenues over five years.

SECTION 4

Focus on Taxes

U.S. Tax System

How It Works

In 1995, the government collected $1.3 trillion dollars. The average federal tax per capita (per person) in the U.S. was $5,108. If, however, we exclude nonworkers – such as children – from our calculations, the average federal tax bill per worker in the U.S. was over $10,000.

The table labeled Federal Income Tax Comparisons shows examples of tax burdens for selected years. Since 1975, taxes have generally decreased because of the large tax cuts of the 1980s.

The individual and corporate income tax schedules given show the tax rate based on income. Federal income taxes are progressive—the higher the income, the greater a percentage of that income paid in taxes.

How Much Do You Pay?

The average American pays more taxes than is often suspected. Mainly because we are taxed in many different ways.

The following is an example provided by the National Taxpayers Union. The NTU figures show that the total tax burden on a family with a median income of $53,000 was approximately $26,000, which amounts to almost 51 percent of earnings. The NTU estimates that 25 percent of earnings goes toward federal taxes, 10.4 percent goes toward state and local taxes, 15 percent goes to indirect taxes (such as gasoline, excise

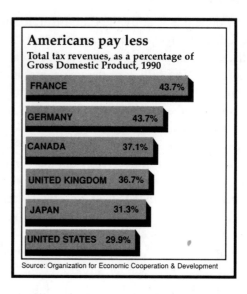

Americans pay less
Total tax revenues, as a percentage of Gross Domestic Product, 1990

FRANCE	43.7%
GERMANY	43.7%
CANADA	37.1%
UNITED KINGDOM	36.7%
JAPAN	31.3%
UNITED STATES	29.9%

Source: Organization for Economic Cooperation & Development

taxes, corporate income taxes, and taxes on production of goods and services).

Although U.S. citizens pay a lot in taxes, we actually have a lower tax burden than other industrialized nations. America's tax revenues as a percentage of GDP are less than those in France, Germany, Japan, the U.K., and Canada.

What's Wrong?

Many argue that our tax system distorts taxpayer choices about consumption and investment. The current system taxes interest on savings, dividends, and capital gains, creating double taxation. As a result, taxes create a bias against investment, favoring current consumption over future consumption, and discouraging saving.

Many also contend that our tax system is too complex, costing at least $40 billion in direct compliance costs and 3 billion hours of taxpayer time. For every $100 of tax revenue taken in, we spend about $1 paying accountants and IRS officials. The IRS is running 11 percent behind last year in processing refunds, which exerts a $4.6 billion drag on the economy.

Reform

Because of the complexity of our tax system and because it discourages investment, many are demanding reform in our tax codes. Republican leaders as well as some Democrats are calling for a radical overhaul of our tax system–not just reform.

This year House Leader Newt Gingrich and Senate Majority Leader Bob Dole appointed Jack Kemp, the former HUD Secretary, to lead a task force that will hold

Cost of Collecting Federal Taxes - 1992	
U.S. Population (in thousands)	256,167
Number of IRS Employees	116,673
Cost to Govt. of Collecting $100 in Taxes	$0.58
Tax per Capita	$4,375.27
Collections by Principal Sources (in thousands of dollars)	$1,120,799,558
Income and Profits Taxes	
Individual	557,723,156
Corporation	117,950,796
Employment Taxes	400,080,904
Estate and Gift Taxes	11,479,116
Alcohol Taxes	NOTE 4
Tobacco Taxes	NOTE 4
Manufacturers' Excise Taxes	NOTE 3
All Other Taxes	33,565,587

NOTE: For fiscal year ending September 30th. NOTE 3: Manufacturers' excise taxes are included in the All other taxes" amount. NOTE 4: Alcohol and tobacco tax collections are now collected and reported by the Bu reau of Alcohol, Tobacco and Firearms. *Source: IRS 1992 Annual Report*

hearings and recommend legislation to simplify the tax system. New plans, both Republican and Democrat, share a political goal: to soothe taxpayer anger by promising to make the tax code both more simple and fairer.

One such plan, proposed by House Minority Leader Dick Gephardt, would retain the familiar progressive income tax while simplifying the methods for filing, as well as encouraging savings and investment.

The Republicans offer a more radical reformation of the tax code. One such plan is the flat tax that would tax salaries and benefits at a single lower rate and eliminate all remaining itemized deductions, from mortgage interest to state and local tax exemptions. Interest, dividends, and capital gains would be tax free for individuals. The flat tax has been proposed by House Majority Leader Dick Armey of Texas and by Senator Arlen Specter of Pennsylvania.

The second Republican plan was offered by Senator Richard Lugar of Indiana. He argued to abolish both the income tax and the IRS in favor of a national retail sales tax collected by the states, because it would encourage savings and decrease fraud.

Another type of national sales tax, proposed by Representatives Bill Archer of Texas and Sam Gibbons of Florida, would tax goods at each stage of production and distribution.

Yet another plan, offered by Senators Sam Nunn of Georgia and Pete Domenici of New Mexico, would keep the familiar income tax, but would permit taxpayers to deduct all savings and investments from the income they declare for tax purposes. Their tax system would be at least as complex as the current system, but it would encourage investment.

Republicans argue that either the sales tax or the flat tax would greatly simplify the tax system and root out tax evasion.

Democratic opponents say the flat tax and the sales tax would mean less taxation for the wealthy. In addition, the sales tax, which taxes consumption, would hurt those who are struggling to buy food and clothing for their families.

1995 Individual/Corporate Tax Rates

There are currently four tax rates for 1995: 15%, 28%, 31%, and 36%. The dollar bracket amounts are adjusted each year for inflation.

Tax Rate	Taxable Income
Single	
15%	$0–22,100
28%	$22,101–53,500
31%	$53,501–115,000
36%	$115,001–250,000

Married Filing Jointly or Widow(er)
15%	$0-36,900
28%	$36,901-89,150
31%	$89,151-140,000
36%	$140,001–250,000

Married Filing Separately
15%	$0–18,450
28%	$18,451–44,575
31%	$44,576–70,000
36%	$70,001–125,000

Head of Household
15%	$0–29,600
28%	$29,601–76,400
31%	$76,401–127,500
36%	$127,501–250,000

There is also a 10% surtax on taxable incomes over $250,000. This provision creates a marginal top tax rate of 39.6%. The maximum tax rate on net capital gains for an individual, estate or trust is 28%.

1993 Corporate Income Tax Rates

Taxable Income	Tax Rate
$0–50,000	15%
$50,001–75,000	25%
$75,001–10 million	34%
Over $10 million	35%

Above $15 million, there is an additonal 5% tax, and above $18.3 million, corporations pay a flat rate of 35%. In addition, personal service corporations (e.g., attorneys, doctors) pay a flat rate of 35%.

Federal Income Tax Comparisons
Taxes at Selected Rate Brackets after Standard Deductions and Personal Exemptions

Adjusted Gross Income	Single return listing no dependents				Joint return listing two dependents			
	1993	*1992*	*1991*	*1975*	*1993*	*1992*	*1991*	*1975*
$10,000	*$593*	*$615*	*$668*	*$1,506*	*-$1,511[2]*	*-$1,384[2]*	*$1,235*	*$829*
$20,000	*2,093*	*2,115*	*2,168*	*4,153*	*236*	*408*	*702*	*2,860*
$30,000	*3,833*	*3,960*	*4,201*	*8,018*	*2,160*	*2,220*	*2,355*	*5,804*
$40,000	*6,633*	*6,760*	*7,001*	*12,765*	*3,660*	*3,720*	*3,855*	*9,668*
$50,000	*9,433*	*9,560*	*9,801*	*18,360*	*5,160*	*5,220*	*5,576*	*14,260*

NOTE: (1) For comparison purposes, tax rate schedules were used. (2) Refund was based on a basic earned income credit for families with dependent children.

What Would You Pay?

Depending on your family circumstances, the various tax alternatives will affect you differently. To see how these systems might affect you, two model families have been created to see how they fare under the different proposals. (Tax rates for the flat tax and sales tax are designed to generate roughly the same revenue as with the current system.)

MARRIED WITH CHILDREN	**EMPTY NESTERS**
• Gross Income of $75,000 • Two children • Large mortgage on home • $10,000 annually from investments	• Gross Income of $75,000 • No children at home • Mortgage completely paid on home • $30,000 annually from investments

CURRENT INCOME TAX

$7,450 — Under the current system, this family falls under the 28% tax bracket. They receive the mortgage interest deduction and exemptions for their children. These exemptions and deductions reduce their tax burden.

This family also falls under the 28% tax bracket; however, because they have fewer exemptions (no children) and fewer deductions (no home mortgage interest deduction), they have a higher taxable income and thus pay more. — **$14,800**

FLAT TAX

Tax rate would be 20% for all earnings.

$10,050 — The flat tax eliminates all of the deductions that this family once took, such as the large home mortgage interest deduction. As a result, this family now pays more in taxes.

Itemized deductions would be eliminated.

This family does better because their income from investments would not be taxed at the personal level. In addition, they do not have many deductions to lose as the other family does. — **$9,025**

U.S.A. INDIVIDUAL INCOME TAX

Tax rate would be slightly higher than the current system.

$7,820 — This type of tax would slightly increase the tax burden of the family, compared to the current system. The increase arises from the inability of the family to take certain deductions.

All savings would, however, be exempt.

Under this proposal, the top tax rate is higher than in the current system. Because this family cannot take many deductions, their tax burden is higher than under the current system. — **$19,560**

NATIONAL SALES TAX

Tax rate on all goods and services would be 19%.

$6,950 — If we assume that the family spends similarly to most families in their income bracket, then we can expect the sales tax burden to be slightly less than with the current system.

The personal income tax would be eliminated.

This family does well under this system because their savings and investments are not taxed. In addition, their high personal income is not taxed. — **$11,680**

Social State of the Nation

Medicare and Medicaid

Background

Over the course of 1995-96, our federal government has been confronted with the pressures of funding Medicare and Medicaid.

As health care costs soar and demands stretch resources, the U.S. faces the impending bankruptcy of these two programs on which so many millions of Americans depend.

Federal spending on the Medicare and Medicaid programs will total $267 billion in 1995. This will account for over 16 percent of the entire federal budget for the year. The combined federal spending on Medicare and Medicaid costs America's taxpayers more than $30 million every hour of every day of the year. Under current conditions, Medicare and Medicaid spending are projected to double every five to seven years.

Medicare: How It Works

Medicare provides for the medical expenses of the elderly and the disabled. A person can receive these funds (1) by being over 65 years of age or disabled and being qualified to receive Social Security or (2) by being older than 65 years of age and by paying a monthly premium ($46.10 in 1995).

Medicare provides such services as:
- in-patient hospital care
- short-term skilled nursing facility care
- home health care
- doctors' services
- diagnostic and lab tests
- outpatient hospital services
- home dialysis
- ambulance services

However, it does not provide for all health care services. Medicare recipients must pay, for instance, up to $700 of their hospitalization fees.

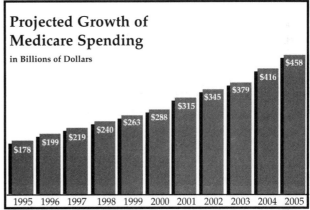

Projected Growth of Medicare Spending
in Billions of Dollars

1995	1996	1997	1998	1999	2000	2001	2002	2003	2004	2005
$178	$199	$219	$240	$263	$288	$315	$345	$379	$416	$458

SOURCE: Congressional Budget Office, April 1995

Medicare was created as a part of Social Security in 1965. The Department of Health and Human Services runs Medicare through a six-member Board of Trustees made up of the Secretary of the Treasury, the Secretary of Labor, the Secretary of Health and Human Services, the Commissioner of Social Security, and two public members.

For most of Medicare's existence it has run surpluses—that is, it has received more income than it paid out for health care claims. Those surpluses had been put into the Hospital Insurance Trust Fund, which presently is worth about $135 billion. In 1996 the Medicare trust fund begins paying out more money in claims than it receives in payroll taxes and by 2002, according to the

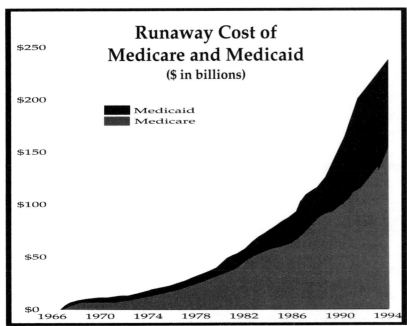

Runaway Cost of Medicare and Medicaid
($ in billions)

■ Medicaid
■ Medicare

Source: Fiscal Year 1996 Budget of the US Government

Congressional Budget Office, this trust fund will be completely used up.

Simply, Medicare will go bankrupt within the next seven years. This means that Medicare will have to be financed by raising taxes or by borrowing. If no changes occur, Medicare alone will take up 18.5 percent of all federal spending.

Medicaid: How It Works

Medicaid provides health care for needy Americans. Unlike Medicare, Medicaid is paid by the federal government as well as state governments. The federal government pays the majority of the burden (57 percent or $89 billion in 1995) but states are in charge of administering the Medicaid programs. To care for the 33 million people whom Medicaid covers, the federal and local governments will spend nearly $175 billion in 1996. Here are some statistics about Medicaid:

• In 1995, 33 million people rely on Medicaid for some form of health care. That means one out of every ten Americans relies on Medicaid.

• One out of every four American children depends on Medicaid for basic care. Children make up about 50 percent of all people who depend on Medicaid. (However, children use up only 15 percent of all Medicare costs.)

• One-third of all births in the U.S. are paid for by Medicaid.

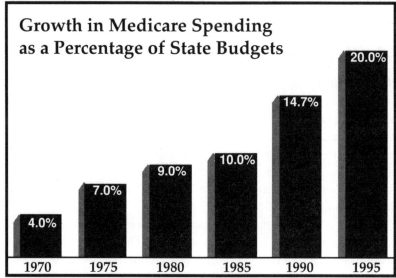

Growth in Medicare Spending as a Percentage of State Budgets

1970	1975	1980	1985	1990	1995
4.0%	7.0%	9.0%	10.0%	14.7%	20.0%

SOURCE:NATIONAL ASSOCIATION OF STATE BUDGET OFFICERS. 1994 STATE EXPENDITURE REPORT

• The disabled and elderly use the majority of Medicaid costs—39 percent and 28 percent, respectively.

Why the Problem Exists

• **Aging Population:** As life expectancy increases and the baby boomers age, the number of people over 65 years of age will sharply increase. The greater demand for Medicare and Medicaid drives up costs.

• **High Health Care Costs:** Researchers and doctors are constantly improving and creating health care services. Increased technology also means increased costs to use these new services. Once again demand increases, resulting in higher costs.

• **Abuse:** Health care professionals often overcharge Medicare and Medicaid because controls are lax. Doctors can either provide services not truly needed by their patients or charge for expensive services never rendered.

Because of the impending bankruptcy of both Medicare and Medicaid and the desire to balance the U.S. budget, both these programs were up for reform in crafting the budget for fiscal year 1996.

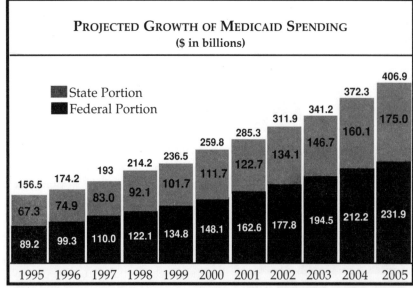

PROJECTED GROWTH OF MEDICAID SPENDING
($ in billions)

■ State Portion
■ Federal Portion

Year	Total	State Portion	Federal Portion
1995	156.5	67.3	89.2
1996	174.2	74.9	99.3
1997	193	83.0	110.0
1998	214.2	92.1	122.1
1999	236.5	101.7	134.8
2000	259.8	111.7	148.1
2001	285.3	122.7	162.6
2002	311.9	134.1	177.8
2003	341.2	146.7	194.5
2004	372.3	160.1	212.2
2005	406.9	175.0	231.9

State spending levels assume average state match of 43%   Source CBO March 1995 Baseline

Medicare Reform

The Congress projects that its new Medicare reform will save the U.S. government $270 billion over the next seven years. The government hopes to realize these savings through the greater use of HMOs (Health Management Organizations) and through increased premiums for all Medicare recipients, particularly for high income recipients.

Those individuals with incomes of at least $75,000 and couples with incomes of more than $150,000 would be forced to pay the highest monthly premiums for Medicare. These recipients would likely pay premiums three times higher than the current premium, $46.10 per month. The average Medicare recipient would also likely experience an increase. By 2002, one could expect to pay approximately $90 per month as a premium.

Although these increased premiums will help save Medicare from bankruptcy, the majority of savings will come as people move into HMOs and other forms of managed care. Lawmakers hope that by sending people to HMOs, they can reduce spending. The idea is that doctors' fees are often lower in managed organizations. In addition, because patients usually see their primary doctor before they go to a specialist, there is a greater chance that abuse of the Medicare system and unnecessary procedures will be avoided.

While lawmakers hope that people will switch into HMOs, the specific bill proposed in Congress provides no direct incentives or pressures for Medicare recipients to switch from visiting the doctors of their choice to enrolling in managed care.

A third area where the government hopes to save comes from imposing a strict system of annual government-set ceilings on Medicare payments to hospitals, doctors, home health care agencies, and laboratories. If spending by health care agencies or doctors exceeded their goal in any given year, the government would cut payments to these health care providers in the

following year. The health plan in total would still allow for substantial growth in spending from $4,800 this year in benefits per recipient to an average of $6,700 per recipient in 2002. Under the current law, Medicare spending would be $8,000 per recipient in 2002. Thus, we can see that the Medicare cuts are merely reducing the rate of growth of Medicare and not reducing Medicare benefits below their current level.

The GOP package, called the Medicare Preservation Act of 1995, is receiving some opposition from the Democrats. Representative Henry Waxman, from California, says, "The plan will destroy the Medicare system as we have known it–in a very few short years." Representative Richard Gephardt of Missouri says that when the people understand what's happening, "they will be outraged."

Responding to complaints, Republican leaders say their plan will offer a vast new world of choices for those enrolled in Medicare. Each year beneficiaries would receive a booklet listing government approved

The GOP Medicare Plan

New choices . . .

Medicare Plus: Private companies offer insurance plans that might feature lower costs than the government program or greater benefits. All plans would have to offer a minimum benefit package equal to that of Medicare.

Medical Savings Account: Beneficiaries could establish a medical savings account. The government would provide a fixed amount of money to the individual who would receive health care coverage through a policy for catastrophic illness. This would yield a lower premium and a higher deductible than the current system. Routine health care costs could be paid from the savings account, and the recipient would be permitted to keep some of the money in the account at the end of the year.

Hospital Coverage: Doctors and hospitals could offer coverage without insurance companies or managed care companies.

Status Quo: If recipients choose to stay with the Medicare program, they can expect to pay slightly higher premiums. Seniors with incomes over $75,000 and couples with incomes over $150,000 will have to pay the largest premiums.

health plans and would be able to choose from a variety of different plans that aren't offered under the current Medicare system. The GOP argues that the majority of cost-cutting will come, not from reducing the benefits of the elderly, but from trying to control health care costs.

Medicaid Reform

In addition to cuts in Medicare, Medicaid will likely receive cuts in fiscal year 1996. Republicans argue that the best way to reform and cut Medicaid is to give block grants to states and allow states to have greater control over forming their Medicaid programs.

The legislation seeks to cut projected Medicaid spending by $182 billion, or 19 percent, over seven years. Republicans in both houses say they are determined to abolish dozens of federal mandates that prescribe, in great detail, who gets what benefits under Medicaid.

However, under the bill, the federal government would set certain amounts of each state's block grant for specific groups: poor women and children, and the disabled and the elderly, including residents of nursing homes. States would have almost complete freedom to set eligibility criteria and define the scope of benefits for each group. The federal government would no longer specify a minimum package of benefits.

The Senate Medicaid bill includes a major source of savings not found in the House bill. It would reduce the number of hospitals that qualify for extra Medicaid payments because they serve large numbers of low-income patients. Such payments, which total $8.5 billion this year, would be reduced to $5 billion from 1996 through 2002. Over the next seven years this change would save $35 billion from the amounts that would be spent under current law.

Proponents argue that giving block grants would be more efficient because states and localities know better what their people need. The federal government would, however, retain some control over the Medicaid program and would encourage states to be more efficient. For instance, in return for accepting smaller block grants, the states would get significantly increased flexibility to run their own programs.

Representative Thomas Bliley Jr., chairman of the House Commerce Committee, hailed the changes, saying they would control the cost of one of the fastest-growing federal benefit programs.

Critics of the plan believe that a block grant approach would increase the number of uninsured, now at 40 million. They are worried that some states may do a worse job than the federal government and would likely not give as much money to Medicaid as is needed.

Representative Henry Waxman of California, who designed much of the current Medicaid program, said this was "a sad day," because there will be "no guarantees of anything" for Medicaid recipients.

Social Security
Background

Signed into law by Franklin Roosevelt in 1935, the Social Security program was created to ensure that the elderly would always have enough money to live on. Since that time, Social Security has become one of the most comprehensive and expensive social programs in the industrialized world.

Workers and their employees each contribute an equal amount to the Social Security program to pay for retirement, disability, and Medicare benefits. Presently, the Social Security tax deducts about 8 percent of earnings from workers.

In 1995, 46 million people received some sort of Social Security benefits. In addition, Social Security accounts for 40 percent of the total income of those over 65 and keeps 38 percent of this group out of poverty.

The two most popular Social Security Programs are OASDI or Old Age Survivors Disability and Health Insurance, and SSI, Supplemental Security Income. More than 40 million people receive monthly OASDI benefits. Of these, the majority are retired workers, nearly 62 percent. Nine percent are disabled workers, 17 percent are survivors of deceased workers, and 12 percent are spouses and children of retired workers.

The average monthly benefit for a male retired worker is approximately $759. The average monthly benefit to a woman retired worker is $548.

The SSI program is administered to approximately 6 million people. SSI is mainly given to the disabled, who comprise 75 percent of the recipients; the other 25 percent goes to the aged. The aged who receive SSI benefits generally receive such benefits because they have very low, if any, earnings or assets.

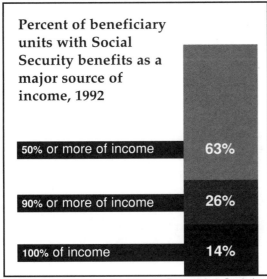

Percent of beneficiary units with Social Security benefits as a major source of income, 1992

50% or more of income — 63%

90% or more of income — 26%

100% of income — 14%

Source:Soc. Sec. Admin. Office of Research & Statistics

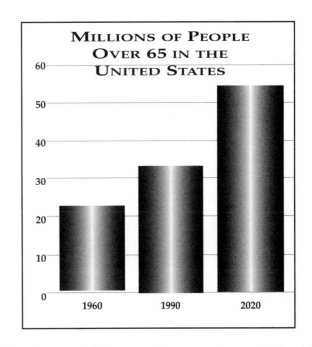

MILLIONS OF PEOPLE OVER 65 IN THE UNITED STATES

1960 1990 2020

Social Security Bankruptcy?

In total, Social Security is presently our most expensive program, costing 22 cents of every dollar of tax revenue. The program will cost American taxpayers approximately $340 billion in 1995.

Because Social Security is our largest program, we can expect it to be targeted when the government has to tackle balancing the budget. Economists tell us that the Social Security program will bankrupt itself around the year 2050.

The problem with Social Security is that we have a growing number of elderly and a shrinking number of younger workers to pay for the benefits of the old. Since 1960, the number of people age 65 and over

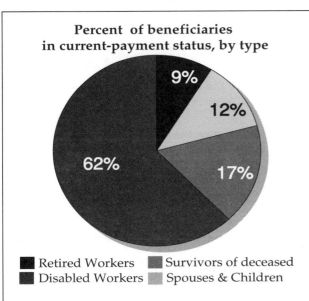

Percent of beneficiaries in current-payment status, by type

9%

12%

62%

17%

■ Retired Workers   ■ Survivors of deceased
■ Disabled Workers ■ Spouses & Children

has increased 89 percent in comparison with the 39 percent growth rate for the total population. The age group 85 and over has grown a tremendous 232 percent.

With the baby boomers (those born between World War II and 1964) reaching old age in the next few decades, the Social Security system faces serious problems. By the time the baby boomers reach retirement, there will be two workers for every senior citizen collecting Social Security.

The Social Security system is a "pay as you go" program, meaning that the elderly are supported not by the payments they themselves made but by the current taxes on young workers. With only two young workers paying for every senior citizen (as compared to fifteen to one when the program first began), we can expect much higher Social Security taxes.

Reform

The government has foreseen some of these problems and has therefore created a Social Security savings account to cover the future claims of baby boomers. Unfortunately, the fund is not enough to cover future claims. In addition, the government has continually borrowed from the Social Security fund to meet other government obligations. In reality, the fund doesn't even really exist. It's just a bookkeeping entry.

To deal with the impending problem, politicians, as

How much will you get back from Social Security?

Your earnings history–whether you have a history of earning a low, average or maximum wage compared to other workers–and your marital status affect your Social Security benefits, as does your retirement age.

In this chart, note that retirees with a history of earning a low wage get a larger share of their preretirement earnings back in benefits each month than do those with histories of average or higher earnings.

Example	Initial monthly benefit			Present value of future benefits			Replacement rate 2		
	Low	Average	Maximum	Low	Average	Maximum	Low	Average	Maximum
Worker (age 65) only	$520	$858	$1,199	$71,000	$118,000	$164,000	58%	43%	24%
Worker and noncontributing spouse	$780	$1,287	$1,798	$127,000	$210,000	$293,000	87%	65%	36%

1 Based on retirement in 1995 at age 65. 2 actual benefit amounts will vary according to a worker's own earning history. Initial benefit as a percentage of preretirement earnings on which Social Security payroll taxes were paid. Source: SSA, Office of the Actuary, June 5, 1995

well as think tanks, have proposed the following solutions:

- A reduction in benefits
- A postponement of benefits
- Increased payroll taxes on upper income workers
- Increased penalties for early retirement
- Reduced benefits for higher income retirees
- A changed benefits formula for future retirees
- Reduced cost of living adjustments and increased taxes on the still smaller portion of working families

The most popular solution politically seems to be a means test by which those people who made a certain amount of income would receive reduced Social Security benefits.

Many economists argue that the entire Social Security system should be reformed, by encouraging people to save now for their retirement, rather than relying on government programs, and to put their money in widely diversified investments for higher returns.

Health Care

Rising Health Care Costs

Part of the large increases in our social programs such as Medicare, Medicaid, and Social Security relate to the rising cost of health care. The United States spends far more per capita on health care than does any other nation on earth. One dollar out of every seven spent goes toward health care.

High spending for health care reflects higher prices for medical services. Increased technology and the increased life span of our people make health care more expensive. Health care costs are also driven up by fraud and the lack of incentives in our system to use health care services wisely.

While health care consumes roughly 20 percent of our gross domestic product, there are nearly 40 million Americans who are not insured at all and even more who get improper health care.

The Uninsured

The majority of the uninsured seem to be young adults and the children of uninsured adults. The uninsured receive insufficient preventative care and often end up flooding our emergency rooms, the most expensive type of health care.

Most Americans are insured through their employers. Employer-provided insurance benefits have increased dramatically since World War II. A recent survey found that more than 25 percent of American households included a family member who stayed in a job because of health coverage.

Many employees pay for increases in health care costs, mainly through lower wages. Many of the uninsured workers employed by small firms earn wages

How Much You Pay for Health Care

Out of Pocket Expenses	$2,280
Health Insurance Costs	
Employer Costs	$3,650
Employee Costs	$1,280
Taxes	$2,930
Total	$10,140

Figures are estimates for 1992. A family is defined as two or more persons related by birth, marriage or adoption and who live together. Figures are estimates for 1992.

Sources: Foster Higgins; Congressional Budget Office; Office of Management & Budget; National Governors' Assoc.; Census Bureau

which, if the wages were reduced by the cost of health insurance, would fall below minimum wage.

Reform

One of Bill Clinton's main campaign promises was to reform the health care system. In 1993, Clinton presented to Congress a 1,342 page bill called the Health Security Act. The bill introduced market forces into the health care system by allowing companies to compete for patients. At the same time, though, the Clinton plan wanted enough federal control to insure universal coverage.

In addition to the opposition that Clinton received in Congress, many lobby groups began a brutal public relations campaign to defeat the Health Security Act. Most vocal was the Health Insurance Association of America (HIAA), representing more than 270 companies that might go bankrupt if the Clinton bill passed.

The HIAA produced publicized television commercials of the fictional Harry and Louise debating the future of health care. Also opposing the Clinton bill was the National Federation of Independent Businesses, representing many small businesses that objected to the Clinton requirement that all companies, even small ones, contribute to their workers' health care costs.

Future of Health Care

The Republicans who now control Congress favor small changes, designed to lower health care costs and increase coverage. These new rules might include restrictions that would forbid insurance companies from denying benefits to patients with pre-existing conditions.

One Republican bill proposed by Representative Bill Thomas of California increases coverage by requiring insurers to offer coverage to all small businesses and individuals who will pay the premiums. In addition, it would forbid insurers to charge the elderly significantly more for insurance than younger people. The bill also increases the portability of insurance, enabling most employees who switch jobs to take their insurance with them. The measure would also limit pain and suffering awards in medical malpractice suits to $250,000.

Other bills to be debated would give people who require long-term medical care tax breaks, encourage small employers to band together and purchase cooperative health insurance, and encourage people to establish medical savings accounts much like IRAs (Individual Retirement Accounts).

One way that politicians are hopeful will reduce the cost is encouraging people to join HMOs or Health Maintenance Organizations. HMOs traditionally limit people to a group of doctors in their area and encourage people to see primary care physicians before seeking more expensive advice from specialists. Many people have begun the trend of joining HMOs because of their lower costs. The trend will likely continue and be encouraged by government.

Because of the Republican commitment to cut the budget, health care will probably not get any additional funds.

Abortion

During his presidency, Bill Clinton has overturned some federal regulations from the Reagan-Bush years making abortion easier to obtain. The Clinton administration also created the Freedom of Access to Clinic Entrances Act, which punishes protestors for using force or threat of force or physically obstructing women seeking abortions.

In the U.S., there are approximately 2,500 clinics where doctors perform 1.6 million abortions annually, totaling one-fourth of U.S. pregnancies. According to a report by the U.S. Centers for Disease Control, women who obtain abortions are predominantly 24 years of age or younger, white, and unmarried. A disproportionate number of black women also receive abortions.

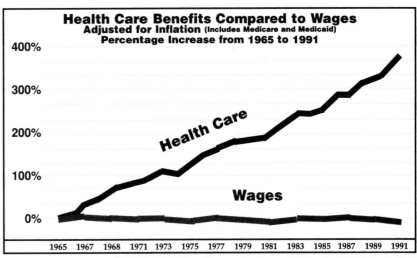

Source: Health Care Financing Administration

New drugs will change abortion debate . . .

The average cost of an abortion is $251. Today abortion is unavailable in 83 percent of U.S. counties, although most women who can afford abortion are able to obtain one. Cities are the homes of most abortion clinics, so rural women must travel long distances to obtain an abortion. Surveys indicate that a large majority of obstetricians and gynecologists are pro-choice, yet many refuse to perform abortions because they feel the work is low paying or against their moral convictions, or because they fear harassment from pro-life protestors.

Two new drugs will soon arrive in the U.S. that may change the face of the abortion issue. RU486, already legal in much of Europe, is a drug which blocks the action of the hormone progesterone, triggering an onset of the menstrual cycle and flushing out the fertilized egg. Taken in pill form, it could be prescribed anonymously by thousands of doctors nationwide. The drug could become available in 1996 if it passes Food and Drug Administration test standards for safety.

In addition, a new drug has entered the picture in 1995. The anticancer agent Methotrexate in conjunction with an anti-ulcer drug was found to safely and effectively induce abortion.

These two abortion drugs could alter the abortion debate. Introducing the drugs would increase the availability of abortion and might increase the number of

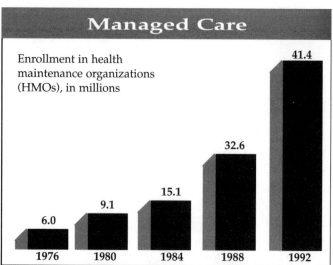

Managed Care

Enrollment in health maintenance organizations (HMOs), in millions

6.0 — 1976
9.1 — 1980
15.1 — 1984
32.6 — 1988
41.4 — 1992

Source: Group Health Association of America

abortions performed. Pro-lifers would likely refocus their protesting on pharmaceutical companies that produce the drugs rather than on abortion clinics.

Disease

Cardiovascular diseases are America's number one killer. More that one in four Americans, over 70 million people, suffer from some sort of cardiovascular disease. Yearly, cardiovascular diseases claim approximately one million lives. Heart disease is about 70 percent more prevalent in men than women. The good news is that due to improved health care habits–decreases in smoking, fat consumption, and alcohol intake–people have reduced their risk of cardiovascular disease.

Cancer is the nation's second leading cause of death. It is characterized as an unrestrained growth of cells. Overall, the rate of cancer incidence and mortality has increased steadily. This is likely due to the increased life expectancy of our population. According to the American Cancer Society, more than eight million Americans are alive who have a history of cancer. The chances of surviving cancer have steadily improved. The American Cancer Society says that survival rate depends on two main factors: how early the cancer is detected, and where the tumor is located. Approximately half a million people die of cancer annually.

Acquired Immune Deficiency Syndrome (AIDS), first discovered in 1981, has claimed the lives of 220,000 Americans. AIDS is

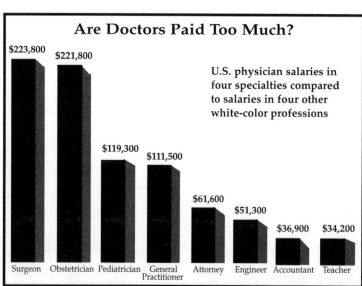

Are Doctors Paid Too Much?

$223,800 — Surgeon
$221,800 — Obstetrician
$119,300 — Pediatrician
$111,500 — General Practitioner
$61,600 — Attorney
$51,300 — Engineer
$36,900 — Accountant
$34,200 — Teacher

U.S. physician salaries in four specialties compared to salaries in four other white-color professions

Source: American Medical Association, American Federation of Teachers

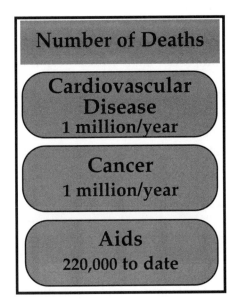

Number of Deaths
Cardiovascular Disease 1 million/year
Cancer 1 million/year
Aids 220,000 to date

caused by the human immunodeficiency virus (HIV), which is spread through contact with infected body fluids such as blood and semen. Infected people may harbor the virus within their bodies for several years or even longer before developing any symptoms.

Regardless of showing symptoms, people who carry HIV can still infect other human beings. The Centers for Disease Control estimates that approximately one million people in the U.S. are infected with HIV.

Although there is no known cure, numerous drugs are being tested, and several have been used to suppress the AIDS virus. Most popular of these drugs is AZT, or azidothymidine.

In the U.S., homosexual and bisexual males make up approximately 54 percent of all adult and adolescent AIDS patients. The other major group afflicted with AIDS is intravenous drug users, who constitute 24 percent of the total.

The overwhelming majority of AIDS cases are found in large cities and metropolitan areas. The disease is spreading faster among heterosexuals than any other group. AIDS is in a tie for sixth place among the leading causes of premature death, but among the six it is the fastest growing, according to the CDC.

Poverty and Welfare

Who Are the Poor?

For several decades, the rate of economic growth reduced the poverty rate. From a historical low of 11.1 percent in 1973, the poverty rate has increased such

that in 1995 it is approximately 14.5 percent. Those who are considered poor are families receiving less than about $15,000 a year. Eight million households fall into this category.

Twelve percent of all U.S. households and 22 percent of all children fall into this poverty range as well as 13 percent of all people over 65. Single-mother households have a greater chance of slipping into poverty than the traditional family or the single-father family. Fifty-two percent of all households in poverty are headed by single mothers.

In addition, the poor have less education than the total population, with only 56 percent finishing high school as opposed to 87 percent finishing high school for the middle class and 97 percent finishing high school in the upper class.

There are some misconceptions about the poor. Many believe the poor have more children than average; however, the average poor family receiving AFDC (Aid to Families with Dependent Children) consists of 2.9 people as opposed to the typical American family, which contains 3.2 people. The majority of the poor, 67 percent, are white; 29 percent are black. Black families tend to be over-represented among the poor.

Surprisingly, roughly one-quarter of the poor do not collect any government benefits at all. Also, fewer than half collect the cash benefits most people think of as welfare, AFDC and SSI. SSI administered by the Social Security Administration.

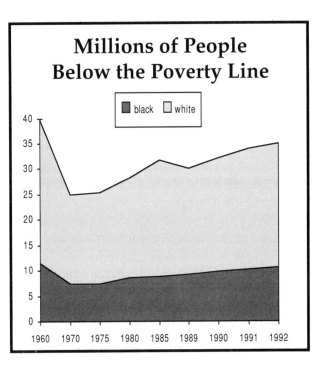

Millions of People Below the Poverty Line

About half of the poor receive Food Stamps and are covered by Medicaid. Only 18 percent live in public or government-subsidized housing. AFDC families tend to get the most benefits, with the amount depending on the state the family lives in. Average monthly benefits for a family of three range from $950 in Alaska to $164 in Alabama. The government says the average AFDC check covers only 63 percent of what states say is needed for their poor families to survive.

The Welfare System

The U.S.'s main welfare programs are Aid to Families with Dependent Children (AFDC), Food Stamps, and subsidized housing. The largest federally funded program is AFDC, which gives benefits to almost 5 million households. The government runs additional programs to help children, including foster care, adoption assistance, and child abuse prevention and treatment.

The government also funds such programs as WIC (Women, Infants and Children), Child and Adult Care Food programs, summer food programs and homeless children nutrition programs—all of which provide funds for child care and nutrition.

Reform

In 1995 and 1996, there is a move to cut the welfare budget in the United States. Many Republicans argue that the best alternative would be to give block grants to states to create their own welfare programs. Specifically, the GOP bill would achieve its goals by replacing dozens of federal programs with five block grants to states. The five grants would cover: cash welfare programs, child welfare programs, child care, school meals, and nutrition programs for women and young children.

Cash Welfare Block Grant

The block grant called Temporary Assistance for Needy Families would essentially replace the current federal program AFDC. The federal government would provide $15.4 billion each year to the states from fiscal year 1996 to fiscal year 2000. The money would be distributed to the states in proportion to each state's share of federal funding in previous fiscal years. Through this program, the number of recipients of funding would likely decrease. In addition, states would have more latitude to run cash welfare programs. The federal government would, however, mandate work requirements for recipients.

Protection Block Grant

This grant would replace 23 federal programs that accounted for $3.6 billion in fiscal year 1994, including foster care, adoption assistance, and child abuse services. The states could use the funds in any way they deemed appropriate, but would have to create citizen review panels to oversee state welfare services. The block grant would total $4.4 billion in fiscal 1996, rising to $5.6 billion in fiscal 2000.

Child Care and Development Block Grant

This block grant would replace nine federal child care programs which provided for child care services for low income families. Again states would be given great flexibility in spending these funds. Federal health and safety regulations for child care would be repealed. The block grant would receive $2.1 billion annually from fiscal years 1996 through 2000.

Family Nutrition Block Grant

This grant would replace nutrition programs such as WIC (Women, Infants and Children), the child and adult care food program, summer food program, and homeless children nutrition program. States would be required to use their funds to provide food to low income pregnant woman, infants, and young children at risk of poor nutrition. States would have the latitude to decide how those services would be administered. Funding for the block grant would be $4.6 billion in fiscal 1996, rising to $5.3 billion in fiscal 2000.

School-Based Nutrition Block Grant

This grant would replace the lunch and breakfast programs, summer food programs, and special milk programs of the school systems. States would be required to fund similar types of programs and would be authorized to spend $6.7 billion in fiscal 1996, rising to $7.8 billion in fiscal 2000.

Aside from giving these block grants, the new welfare system would also scale back the Food Stamp program. The government would provide a cap for food stamps. This means that if the number of applicants for food stamps increased, all recipients would receive proportionately less benefits. The bill restricts both illegal and legal aliens from certain public benefits such as supplemental security income (SSI), cash welfare, social service block grant funds, Medicaid, and food stamps. The bill would also alter eligibility requirements for SSI and the cash benefit program for the blind, dis-

The Welfare System

Program	# of Recipients (thousands)	Total Cost (millions)
AFDC	14,144	$22,286
Food Stamps	28,400	24,800
School Lunch	24,600	3,856
School Breakfast	4,900	787
WIC	5,400	1,958
Child and Adult Care	1,800	966
Summer Feeding	1,900	182
Elderly Nutrition	245	145
Total Cost		**$ 54,980**

abled, and elderly. Drug addiction and alcoholism, for instance, would no longer be considered a disability

Welfare Reform

Will . . .

♦ **Give States More Control**
Block grants will be given by the federal government to states in order to run welfare programs.

♦ **Reduce Eligibility**
Immigrants and certain disabled children will no longer be eligible to receive funds. In addition, after a certain period, those receiving welfare will be required to work.

♦ **Reduce Welfare Spending**
Nearly every welfare program from Food Stamps to nutrition programs will not grow as fast as is currently dictated by our current welfare program.

♦ **Require Fathers and Mothers to Provide Child Support**
Those who do not will risk legal action and suspension of driver's license.

under the program. In addition, disabled children could receive benefits only if they were confined to a hospital. The bill would also create new state and federal agencies which would help find parents who fail to pay child support. While the bill has yet to pass through Congress and receive the president's approval, it is likely that this bill or a very similar one will pass in fiscal year 1996.

The Republican welfare plan would save about $70 billion over the next seven years.

The Republicans argue that states and localities know best what their people need, and thus would act more efficiently. Opponents to this bill argue that states are often remiss in allocating money correctly. Others point out that they may just be shifting problems from the federal level to the state level. Susan Steinmetz, a welfare analyst at the Center on Budget and Policy

Priorities, a bilateral research group, said, "Amid all the debate and federal amendments, we shouldn't lose sight of the fact that this bill is cutting spending, sending problems back to states without the resources to address them." Opponents point to the failure of previous legislation which has given states rights.

In 1998, the federal government created a bill which required more than half of the nation's AFDC recipients to participate in a state-run Job Opportunities and Basic Skills training (JOBS) program.

Four years later, however, only 16 percent of those eligible were participating in JOBS, mainly because states could not or would not allocate their 40 percent share of the expense to run the training programs.

Opponents of the new Republican bill say something similar might happen if states were given block grants. States would no longer be required to put up their own money to obtain federal funds and likely many needy people would be turned away by their state governments.

Many Democrats are certainly fighting the welfare reform proposed by the Republicans. Others are working for some sort of compromise. Because so many of the American people feel that welfare reform is necessary, most politicians are eager to pass some kind of restructuring.

Education

Public Education System

Over 60 million students and approximately 5 million teachers, administrators, and support staff are directly involved in our public education. Nearly $400 billion is spent annually by the federal government as well as state and local governments to run our public education system. This accounts for nearly 8 percent of the gross domestic product and equals spending $6,000 per student.

State and local governments take in the most revenue for public education, each spending about 47 percent of all money spent on education. In contrast, the federal government only spends 6.2 percent of all the money spent on public education.

How We Compare

Despite our high spending compared to other industrialized nations, America still lags behind most of the industrialized countries in high school and elementary school achievement. According to studies, U.S. children fall behind their peers in Japan, Germany, France, and Korea in math, science, and geography.

While our high school and elementary education is lacking, our college level education is considered the best in the world as many students from other nations come to study at our top universities.

In general, Americans are becoming more educated. Eighty-one percent of them finished high school and nearly 45 percent have had some years of college.

Another important trend in education is that education has become a determining factor in the level of wealth that one attains. Those without a high school degree are six times more likely to end up below the poverty line. Those with a college degree are more likely to end up in the middle class or in upper levels of the income distribution.

Reform

In order to reduce costs and improve the quality of our education, many argue that reform is needed. Among the plans for reform are: (1) to increase competition by giving grants to families to choose a public or private school for their children; (2) to raise standards for becoming a teacher; (3) to eliminate administration and give more power to teachers; and (4) to encourage private business to help in training at school.

As the Congress looks for ways to cut the budget, education is among those programs to be looked at. The House has proposed a bill which would end the

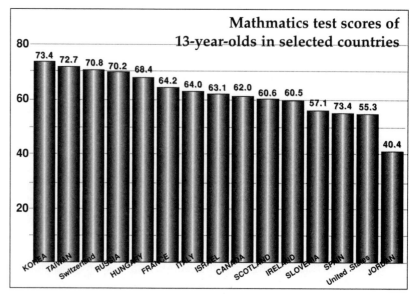

Mathmatics test scores of 13-year-olds in selected countries

Country	Score
KOREA	73.4
TAIWAN	72.7
Switzerland	70.8
RUSSIA	70.2
HUNGARY	68.4
FRANCE	64.2
ITALY	64.0
ISRAEL	63.1
CANADA	62.0
SCOTLAND	60.6
IRELAND	60.5
SLOVENIA	57.1
SPAIN	73.4
United States	55.3
JORDAN	40.4

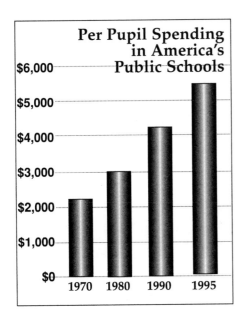

Per Pupil Spending in America's Public Schools

interest subsidy in the Stafford Student Loan Program. The interest subsidy allows a six-month window after graduation where no interest charges would accumulate for a student loan. The proposed cutbacks from ending the interest subsidy would save $12.4 billion over the next five years. The House and Senate, however, do not propose to end the Stafford Loans nor would they make students pay back money until after graduation.

The GOP argues that ending the interest subsidy would not harm students. A student taking out a four-year maximum loan of $17,000, for instance, would pay $252 rather than $208 per month.

College Education

The average cost of college is rising at a fast rate. The cost of tuition, mandatory fees, college room and board at a four-year private college was approximately $15,000 per year. This is a 200 percent increase since 1980.

Four-year public colleges ran approximately $6,000 for state residents, and $11,000 for nonresidents. This is a 214 percent increase since 1980.

Number of Degrees Conferred Annually	
Bachelor's	1,178,000
Professional	75,100
Master's	377,000
Doctorate	41,300

Two-year public colleges cost about $2,000 for state residents and $4,000 for nonresidents. The high price of college education is beginning to strain middle class families who often do not qualify for college aid.

Immigration
Who Are Immigrants?

Today immigration accounts for approximately 33 percent of all U.S. population growth. With the dramatic decline in our birth rates and fertility rates, the United States may well begin to experience negative population growth by the year 2030. In fact, according to the Office of Population Research at Princeton University, the United States will need a half million immigrants to keep our population at its current levels.

Approximately half a million people immigrate to the U.S. annually and the majority of them are from two general areas of the world, Central America and East Asia. The number of immigrants entering the United States has increased steadily since the early 1960s, from 1.5 million in 1960–1964 to 5.6 million in 1985–1990. About 8 percent of the nation's population is foreign-born, the highest proportion in the past four decades.

A 1992 immigration law sets the limits for the number of immigrants entering the U.S. per year. In addition, it also restricts those coming as family sponsored immigrants.

Regardless of these laws, though, there are many immigrants who come to the United States illegally. Over the past several years immigration has been at the forefront of political debate. As immigrants from China, Haiti, Cuba, and Central America leave their countries

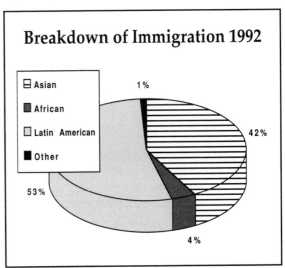

Breakdown of Immigration 1992

☐ Asian
■ African
☐ Latin American
■ Other

Top 6 States Admitting Immigrants	
California	34%
New York	14%
Florida	8%
Texas	8%
New Jersey	5%
Illinois	5%

and come to American cities, constituents have become increasingly concerned about America's ability to cope with the immigrant problem.

Anti-Immigrant Sentiment

In states where there are large immigrant populations, people fear that immigrants may take many public benefits. In California for instance, Proposition 187, a law which would prevent immigrants from using many public benefits, was proposed and fought for by important political leaders such as California governor Pete Wilson. While Proposition 187 was ruled unconstitutional, there is still an anti-immigrant feeling among voters and a desire to curtail much of the immigration now coming to America.

Those who argue against immigration say that immigrants take jobs from U.S. workers and soak up too many government services. Others argue that the U.S. has an obligation to political refugees and that immigration provides the U.S. with cultural diversity and a stronger work force.

Reform

The budget for fiscal year 1996 incorporates proposals that would increase funding for the Immigration and Naturalization Service by $2.6 billion. The increase in funds for immigration would be used for three major plans: (1) border control and management, (2) interior enforcement, and (3) the removal of deportable aliens.

In addition, a proposed border services user fee would generate $200 million in 1996, would help INS in customs facilitate border crossings, and improve border management.

In order to help states with the burdens of illegal immigration, the budget proposes $300 million to help cover costs associated with incarcerating criminal ille-

gal aliens, $150 million to cover some of the emergency medical costs of undocumented immigrants under Medicaid, and $100 million to help school districts with high numbers of immigrant students.

In 1995, the administration had also taken unprecedented steps to deter illegal immigration with its border patrols such as Operation Hold the Line in El Paso, Texas, and its Operation Gatekeeper in San Diego.

Homelessness, Crime, and Suicide

Homelessness

Both policy experts and the citizenry as a whole seem to be less optimistic than they once were that the homeless problem can be eradicated. In 1987, the Urban Institute made an estimate of 500,000 to 600,000 homeless in America. The U.S. Bureau of the Census found a total of 178,828 persons in emergency shelters for the homeless and 49,793 persons visible at pre-identified street locations during a special count in 1990.

About 25 percent of all these homeless families are headed by women who left home to escape domestic violence. Another 50 percent of the homeless are single men. About 20 percent of the homeless are employed in full- or part-time jobs and another 25 percent are veterans.

Many homeless are drug abusers and an even greater number are mentally ill. Leading causes of homelessness, according to a survey of mayors, are: lack of affordable housing, domestic violence, unemployment, drug abuse, and teen pregnancy.

Congress appropriated approximately $1 billion last year to deal with the homeless problem, yet cities and towns continue to pay the majority of the bill. New York City reports that it spends about $500 million each year on services for the homeless.

Crime

By the number of crimes reported in the U.S., the United States tops the list as the world's most violent democracy. Crime, drugs, joblessness, and welfare dependency are sapping the strength of America's inner cities. Cities are struggling with crime, inadequate budgets, and a disintegrating family structure.

Since 1983 the number of rapes has increased by 38

percent, robberies by 32 percent, murder by 23 percent, and violent crimes by a staggering 54 percent.

Almost 66 percent of all murders in the United States are committed with guns. Handguns alone account for more than half the murders. About 80 percent of all teenage homicides are the result of a firearm injury.

The number of Americans in jail or prison has doubled in the last eight years and has increased about 150 percent in the last eleven. For every 20 people in the U.S., there is one arrest.

In fiscal year 1991, the U.S. spent more than $20.1 billion on penal corrections, including operations and construction, up 20 percent from the previous year. Still, the prisons are overcrowded, operating at 52 percent over capacity.

In 1994, after much debate, the U.S. Congress passed a crime bill which increased funding to hire more policemen, put a ban on certain assault weapons, tightened the parole system, and gave money to social programs aimed at reducing crime including sports and education programs. The bill was not supported by the majority of Republicans in Congress, basically because of the assault weapons ban and the costs of social programs.

Child Abuse

In recent years, experts have declared that child abuse and neglect were epidemic. Cases of neglect have overflowed our hospitals, foster care homes, social worker case loads, and court dockets. About 2.4 million cases of child abuse, child sexual abuse, and child neglect are reported to child protective agencies each year. Since 1990, reports of child abuse have quadrupled. Furthermore, it is estimated that nearly 2 million children under age 18 are affected in some way by the substance abuse of their parents.

Drugs

A study released by the U.S. Department of Health and Human Services in 1990 estimated that drug abuse costs the U.S. $58.3 billion a year. The rate of illicit drug use remains higher for American youth than for the youth of any other industrialized country. Drug use has remained fairly constant over the past four years, with slight increases in the use of LSD and heroin.

The most used drug is alcohol. A 1988 National Health Interview Survey reported that 15.3 million Americans exhibit symptoms of alcohol abuse or dependence such as binge drinking and loss of control.

Another popular drug is tobacco. Approximately 400,000 people die each year from diseases caused by smoking. Among adults, smoking has decreased but smoking among young people has remained fairly constant.

Suicide

According to the National Center for Disease Control and Prevention, between 1980 and 1992 the overall teenage suicide rate increased by 28 percent. Deaths involving firearms accounted for more than three-fourths of the overall increase. Among children between 10 and 14, suicide remains rare, but even in that tender age range the overall rate increase was 125 percent. In 1993, there were approximately 31,000 reported suicides.

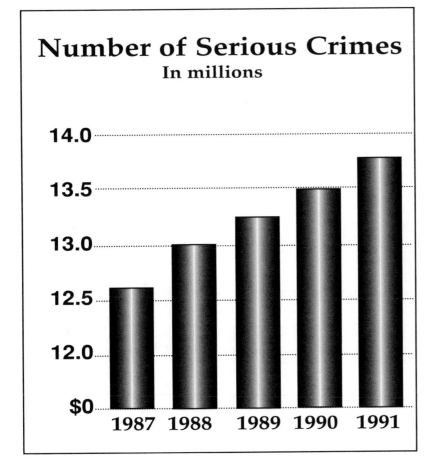

Number of Serious Crimes
In millions

Economic State of the Nation

Debt and Deficit

How Big Is the Debt?

Presently, the debt is over $4 trillion. The debt can be defined as the accumulation of all of our deficits. In other words, it is the amount that we have continually borrowed and that we owe to both our citizens and to foreign lenders. Many have tried to explain to us just how large the national debt is. Stephen Moore, author of *Government: America's Number One Growth Industry*, provides the following examples:

"If Congress paid down the deficit a dollar every second, it would take 130,000 years, or roughly the amount of time that has passed since the Ice Age, to pay down the present debt."

Here's another example: "If you laid the debt out in dollars from end-to-end, it would reach out into space four times the distance between the earth and the sun." Any way you look at it, the amount that the U.S. government owes is nearly unfathomable.

Debt Growth

The deficits which began to be so high throughout the '80s and into the '90s exist for two reasons. The first has to do with the dramatic rise in our federal government spending. Since 1960, the government has grown faster than any other segment of the American economy. The government now consumes about 25 percent of the gross domestic product of the U.S. It is estimated that by the year 2010, that number will shoot above 30 percent.

The largest growing sector of the government is entitlement spending. Entitlement spending consists of programs such as health care, Social Security, Medicare, Medicaid, and other types of income security.

The deficit has also risen because of the tax cuts which occurred in the 1980s. Because of these tax cuts, revenues did not keep pace with spending. There is and will likely continue to be controversy about how exactly the Reagan tax cuts affected the growth of the deficit and the debt. However, we can say with certainty that the tax cuts did nothing to reduce the deficit and more than likely aggravated the problem.

The Cost of Living with Debt
Low Growth Rate

For the past two decades, our growth rate has hovered around 2.5 percent, a sharp decline from the 3.5 percent to 4.0 percent pace averaged in the post–World War II era. If the economy had grown over the past twenty years at the same pace that it did after the war, the average American household would have an income at least $12,000 higher than it is today.

National Debt
1995

Debt held by the public:
$3,432,213,000,000

Debt held by gov't trust funds:
$1,211,498,000,000

Total National Debt:
$4,643,711,000,000

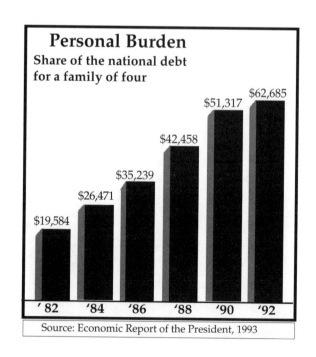

Personal Burden
Share of the national debt for a family of four

$19,584 — '82
$26,471 — '84
$35,239 — '86
$42,458 — '88
$51,317 — '90
$62,685 — '92

Source: Economic Report of the President, 1993

Many economists believe that the major cause of our low growth rate is the fact that we as a people save very little. Part of our low savings rate has to do with large debt and deficit. Every year the government must encourage people to buy its bonds to finance the deficit. This financing cost draws money away from the private sector and puts it into the public sector. Therefore, not only does the government not invest in its future by saving, but it also draws money away from the private sector.

If the United States continues as it has been for the past two decades with approximately a 2.5 percent growth rate, we can expect that our per capita personal income will be approximately $40,000 in 2020 and $65,000 in 2040. Compare that with what we would have with a 4 percent growth rate (the growth rate we had at the end of World War II): $60,000 in 2020 and $130,000 in 2040.

We can learn from this experiment that a couple of points in growth rate can make a huge difference in the long run. America's growth rate lags behind that of other industrialized nations, such as Japan or Germany. This means people of these other nations are becoming richer at a faster pace than Americans.

Lost Money on Interest

Another drawback in living with a debt is that the U.S. has to pay interest on that debt. The third largest expense for the government is now paying interest on the debt. When the government borrows money it has to pay the money back with interest just as an individual or corporation does. In 1995, that interest was approximately $250 billion, which is over four times the amount the federal government spends on education.

Generational Inequity

By running such high deficits and increasing our debt, we are borrowing from future generations. Even-

Your earnings would grow much faster if America saved		
Growth Rate	Average Personal Income	
	2020	2040
2.5%	$40,000	$65,000
4.0%	$60,000	$130,000

DRAWBACKS OF LIVING WITH DEFICITS AND DEBT

- Higher Interest Rates
- Lower Investment
- Lower Growth Rate
- Lost Revenue to Pay Interest on Debt
- Being a Debtor to Foreign Countries
- Large Burdens on Future Generations
- Long-term Decrease in the Standard of Living

tually someone will have to pay for the debt which we have accumulated, as well as suffer our low growth rates.

The Congressional Budget Office projects that children may face as much as 82 percent tax rates if we continue to spend as we are today.

One economist, Allen Auerbach from the University of California at Berkeley, calculated that in 1990, a 70-year-old man would receive net benefits from the government over his lifetime of $46,000. In contrast, a 25-year-old man can expect to make net payments over his lifetime of $226,000.

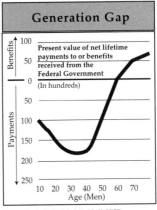

Generation Gap

Present value of net lifetime payments to or benefits received from the Federal Government (In hundreds)

Source: Auerbach, Gochale & Kotlikoff, OECD

Such figures demonstrate that huge transfers from the future generations are being made to the present generations—leaving future generations with high taxes, fewer benefits, and lower growth rates.

The U.S. is not the only nation which is transferring debt to future generations. Germany, Italy, and Sweden are among other nations that are creating large future obligations.

Even Japan, with its graying population and large state pension liabilities, will face crisis. Estimates indicate that Japan's net-debt-to-GDP ratio will jump from an estimated 13 percent this year to more than 300 percent in 2030. In contrast, America's is only forecast to rise from 38 percent to 100 percent over the same period.

Is Debt the Right Measure?

Many argue that the debt is not a good measure of America's future obligations. In order to get a true gauge of our obligations one also has to account for our future commitments such as Social Security benefits. Proponents for this measure argue that this method is more realistic and is consistent with GAAP (Generally Agreed-upon Accounting Principles). These figures, along with the Balance Sheet, are presented in the *Financial Review* section.

America's Vital Signs
GDP Growth

Gross domestic product (GDP) increased at an annual rate of 2.8 percent, or $37.9 billion, in the first quarter of 1995, to bring us to a GDP of $5.47 trillion, the Commerce Department has reported. The GDP growth seems to have dropped from the last quarter of 1994, when it grew at 5.1 percent. This slow growth in 1995 represents the slowest quarter since the summer of 1993.

The Commerce Department's report is consistent with its soft landing scenario or the notion that the economy is slowing to a noninflationary sustainable pace. Economists seem to believe that from now on the economy will grow at a slow rate hovering around 2.5 percent. They argue that we are now at full capacity, meaning that most people in the U.S. are employed and that trying to push our growth higher would only cause inflation.

Regardless of economists' warnings, many analysts are predicting that activity will pick up throughout 1995, perhaps enough to warrant further monetary tightening by the Federal Reserve. The Federal Reserve has targeted a growth rate of 2.5 percent for the U.S. in order to maintain growth and at the same time restricting inflation.

The U.S. Dollar

Throughout the '80s, many economists felt that the dollar had been overvalued. This made it cheap for Americans to buy foreign products and expensive for foreigners to buy American products. Recently, though, the dollar has been on the decline.

Two factors accounting for the dollar's devaluation are: (1) Many U.S. dollars have been flooding out of Latin American due to a lot of instability in the region, and looking for some other safe haven; (2) Declining U.S. interest rates relative to those in Europe and Japan have fostered the flow of short-term cash out of dollars into yen and marks.

The fall of the U.S. dollar has caused trouble abroad. A declining dollar encourages foreigners to buy American. European and Asian currencies have been on the rise in comparison to the United States dollar.

The U.S. has shown no large effort to try to prop up the dollar. The government did at one point authorize the Federal Reserve to purchase U.S. dollars on world currency markets. Regardless of this action, though, the U.S. dollar has continued to fall in comparison to many other currencies.

Despite other countries' urgings, it seems that the U.S. will not risk jeopardizing its own expansion (which is now in the fifth year of growth without price pressures and without inflation). The U.S. is hoping the devaluation of the dollar will force nations like Germany and Japan to loosen their highly restrictive monetary policies and allow American imports to enter their nations.

Other Measures of Growth

Other reports by the Commerce Department show that movement in inventory is down, as is consumer spending. Consumer spending grew by just 1.4 percent

INDICATORS

	1994	1995	1996	1997	1998
% change, 4th Qtr to 4th Qtr					
Real Gross Domestic Product	3.1	3.0	2.9	2.8	2.7
Consumer Price Index	2.9	3.0	3.0	3.0	3.0
Calendar Year Average					
Unemployment Rate	6.2	5.7	5.4	5.3	5.3
Interest Rate 91-day Treasury Bills	4.2	4.4	4.4	4.4	4.4
Interest rate 10-year Treasury Notes	6.1	6.0	6.0	6.0	6.0

in the first part of 1995, compared with 5.7 percent in the previous quarter and 4.3 percent in the third quarter of 1994. In contrast, business inventories grew by $63 billion in the first part of 1995. While many economists were expecting greater inventory growth, this growth was still substantial.

Export growth was very sluggish the beginning of 1995, at only 0.6 percent. This was a dramatic drop in the growth rate, from 20.2 percent in the final quarter of 1994. The Commerce Department, however, reports that some of this drop can be attributed to the Mexican peso crisis. Exports to Mexico dropped because the Mexican people faced a devaluation of the peso and economic crisis.

The projections for the rest of the year for exports seem good. The U.S. dollar has fallen in comparison to the yen, the mark, and many other European currencies. Furthermore, there is evidence that the economies of other European and Asian nations are coming out of hard times and will likely be able to spend more on U.S. goods. In general, the government is expecting U.S. exports to grow by a strong 12.5 percent this year.

On another good note, investment in business has been growing at an annual rate of 13.7 percent. Most economists believe that this growth will continue throughout 1995. Residential housing, on the other hand, has fallen by 6.6 percent as many speculators are halting their projects because they project slower economic growth.

On the whole, indicators provide a mixed review. Economists are saying that our growth in GDP will be somewhere between 2 percent and 4 percent this year.

The Savings Rate

One concern about the American economy is the low savings rate compared to that of many industrialized countries. Because of the lower U.S. savings rate, there is less money available for investment. Generally, when someone wants to start a new business or a new venture, he must rely on the funds available in U.S. banks to do so. Because the American people save very little and because our U.S. government is running deficits, there is very little money available for investment. Essentially that means that the U.S. will have and does have slower growth rates than those countries that save more.

Historically, since the early '70s, savings and investment rates in the U.S. have been very low. Because of this, our real productivity growth has averaged less than 1 percent per year–not enough to double our living standard every 80 years. This tremendous slowdown in our nation's productivity is the main reason real wages and living standards have stagnated.

In some cases, living standards have declined for Americans. For this reason, many politicians, economists, and analysts have argued that we must balance our federal budget and reform our tax system in a way that would help increase savings and investments in the U.S. If a plan is undertaken properly, many argue this would lead to higher wages and living standards for most Americans.

Quality of Life

Has the American quality of life increased or decreased in the past decade? New research from professor of economics and author of *The American Economy* Herbert Stein shows that since 1980 American families' incomes have risen. Incomes did not rise so fast as they did between 1955 and 1973, but they grew at a respectable real rate of about 2 percent.

Many economists, however, argue that most of this rise in income can be attributed to women's entering the workforce and adding a second income to the family. They argue, therefore, that people are working harder for the same income and in some cases for less income.

Labor Statistics

Unemployment

Throughout 1995 unemployment has hovered around 5.7 percent. Since pulling out of the recession in April

1991, the U.S. has done a good job at decreasing the unemployment rate.

However, in April and May 1995, the economy started losing jobs. In May more than 100,000 jobs were lost. This was the largest setback since our nation began pulling out of the recession.

The loss in jobs surprised the Labor Department, which had forecast an increase in employment of around 175,000 jobs in May. The reaction to the loss in jobs was mixed. Some perceived it as a sign that the U.S. would not overheat the economy and increase inflation. Others saw it as a negative signal indicating a significant slowdown in economic growth. Whether or not the loss in jobs will be a trend is unknown. At present, the unemployment rate does not seem to be increasing and remains stable at 5.7 percent.

Labor Costs

Average hourly labor costs in the U.S. and in France are roughly equal at $17.50, according to research done by the Swedish Employers Confederation. In the U.S., most of the $17.50 goes toward wages for time worked; $3.50 goes to taxes, and only $1.00 to holiday time. In France, $5.00 goes to Social Security and other taxes, and $3.00 goes for holiday time.

Germany has the highest hourly wages, more than $27.00. However, a greater percentage of their income goes toward taxes. Japan's holiday bonus pay tops the list at almost $6.00 an hour, or 27 percent of the hourly rate of $22.00.

The cost for employee benefits in the U.S. has been rising. A survey done by the U.S. Chamber of Commerce showed that benefits, including Social Security and other payroll taxes, holidays and vacations, now account for about 42 percent of payroll costs. Employers spend an average of $14,807 on employee benefits.

Workers' benefits have been increasing for a number of reasons. Corporate restructuring has resulted in increases in benefit costs, as well as increases in permanent layoffs and early retirement buyouts. In addition, health care insurance has contributed to the rising cost of benefits.

Although the costs of employee benefits are rising, they are still not so high as in many other industrialized countries, particularly in Western Europe.

Growing Inequality

Since the 1970s, inequality in income has been on the rise. Presently, we have the widest rich-poor gap since

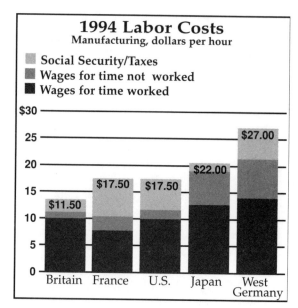

1994 Labor Costs
Manufacturing, dollars per hour

the U.S. Census Bureau began keeping track of these statistics in 1947. The top one-fifth families now earn 44.6 percent of all income in the U.S., compared to 4.4 percent of income for the bottom fifth. The national income of the richest 5 percent of Americans rose from 18.6 percent in 1977 to 24.5 percent in 1990, while the share for the poorest Americans fell.

A variety of reasons may contribute to this increasing inequality.

First, a less progressive tax system allowed the rich to keep more of their income and did not redistribute money to the poor.

In addition, there is now a greater premium put on

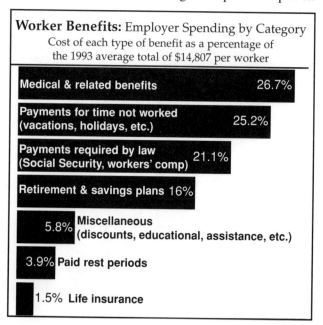

Worker Benefits: Employer Spending by Category
Cost of each type of benefit as a percentage of the 1993 average total of $14,807 per worker

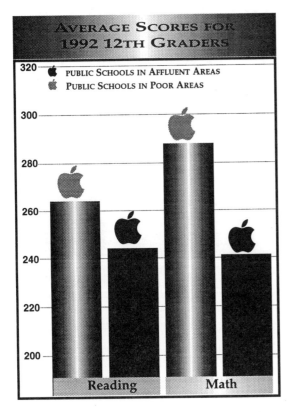

AVERAGE SCORES FOR 1992 12TH GRADERS

PUBLIC SCHOOLS IN AFFLUENT AREAS
PUBLIC SCHOOLS IN POOR AREAS

Reading   Math

education. More-educated workers became more highly paid, while less-educated were paid less.

Presently, there is less demand for blue-collar workers than in the past. Import competition and immigration have sent blue-collar jobs abroad. Furthermore, technology has made other blue-collar jobs unnecessary.

Business Week reported in August 1994, "The well-paying blue-collar jobs that gave U.S. workers rising living standards for most of this century are vanishing. Today you can all but forget about joining the middle class unless you go to college."

Furthermore, most evidence suggests that the majority of college-bound children come from middle- to upper-class families. Not surprisingly, these children make higher scores on standardized tests. This means that these college-educated children will likely remain in the upper class, while the children of the poor who do not attend college will likely remain poor because of their lack of education.

How big of a problem is inequality? Some economists argue that we should not worry so much about inequality as we should about the overall growth of the economy. Others argue that inequality can actually hinder growth because it destroys the middle class and because it inspires doubt in the system. Still others argue that the U.S. has a moral obligation to maintain a certain level of equality.

Growing Gap Between the Rich and the Poor

Income Level	Share of National Income		Average Family Income		% Change
	1980	**1992**	**1980**	**1992**	
Top 25%	48.2%	51.3%	$78,844	$91,368	up 15.9%
Second 25%	26.9%	26.3%	$44,041	$46,471	up 5.5%
Third 25%	17.3%	16.0%	$28,249	$28,434	up 0.7%
Bottom 25%	7.6%	6.5%	$12,359	$11,530	down 6.8%

International State of the Nation

Foreign Policy

Defining a New Strategy

Ever since the end of the cold war in the late '80s, America has been struggling to redefine its foreign policy. The old order of the bipolar world which kept ethnic tensions in check for so many years no longer exists. The globe is torn by ethnic wars and civil unrest: Bosnia, Somalia, Rwanda, the Middle East, and throughout the former Soviet republics. As 1995 ends, there are more than three dozen trouble spots around the globe—either now in open conflict or ready to fight at the slightest provocation.

Amidst the turmoil, America debates how to react. Should America remain the protector of human rights and freedom for the world? And if we should, what groups should we support in the various civil wars that are raging all over the globe? Should we merely send troops to keep the peace as we did in Somalia? Should we allow our troops to attack as we did in the Gulf War? If we do engage, will the American people be willing to give up not only valuable resources that could be used domestically but also the lives of our soldiers?

The New World Order

However we decide to act in the future, we will have to consider certain trends that are shaping the international scene.

1. It will become increasingly difficult to separate our domestic and foreign policy. As we grow more and more dependent on other nations for our economy, we must realize that our foreign policy will often shape our standard of life at home. A quarter of America's economy depends on foreign trade. Most of our recent growth has been driven by our exports. The United States is the world's largest trading nation and largest debtor nation. Thus, our economic stability at home depends on our foreign policy.

2. We must realize that our international economic policy and our international security policy depend on one another. Traditionally, America's presence abroad has been secured by a military relationship with countries throughout Europe and Asia. In order to pursue our economic agenda we must also consider our military involvement in these areas. Conversely, in order to make decisions about our military involvement in these areas, we must also consider the economic ramifications.

3. The United States must balance interests among various different regions. The Pacific rim area—most notably, Japan, South Korea, Singapore, and Thailand—has provided increasingly large markets for the United States. However, the U.S. still invests a majority of its international funds in Western Europe. Our ambassadors must, therefore, balance the new emerging markets throughout Asia, Latin America, and Africa, while maintaining long-term commitment of trade with Western Europe.

4. The United States must face choosing to act in international conflicts either unilaterally or multilaterally. In U.S. actions in Bosnia, as well as other trouble spots in the world, will we be willing to take action by ourselves, or will we try to act through the United Nations?

5. The U.S. must be equipped to encounter new powers such as Russia and China. Both are in the midst of volatile transitions and are destined for some sort of political power by virtue of their large populations, growth rates, and technological advances. Russia and China are both

FY 1995 Unfunded Contingency Costs for Defense

- $1,040.5 Southwest Asia
- $594.6 Haiti
- $367.1 Cuba
- $311.9 Bosnia
- $89.0 Maintenance of Troops Abroad
- $59.1 Recovery of Troops Abroad
- $59.0 Korea
- $17.3 Somalia
- $17.2 Rwanda

TOTAL COSTS
in millions
$2,555.7

already nuclear powers with agendas of their own. Neither is instinctively democratic and relationships with them will be difficult.

America's Defense

To meet the challenges of the new world order, America must redirect its military to deal with ethnic and civil wars. Since the end of the cold war, the U.S. military has tried to transform itself from an entity capable of conducting a complete nuclear war against the Communist world to an entity able to launch small, fast, conventional units for peacekeeping in distant lands. We must be ready for a variety of different terrains and conflicts. In a world where trouble could spring up anywhere, our greatest weakness is not knowing our enemy.

During fiscal 1995 and 1996, America has been involved in a number of local disputes throughout the globe. The United States usually pays most of the money to maintain U.N. peacekeeping troops in various areas.

Furthermore, as many military strategists point out, coming wars will be wars of technology. In the future, our enemies may introduce viruses into our computers rather than launching bombs at our shores. They may genetically engineer diseases or intercept our communications with satellites. These are the kinds of attacks that America must be capable of combating.

Amidst a need for transformation, the military has had to deal with large budget cuts. By 1997, the defense budget will have suffered reductions greater than

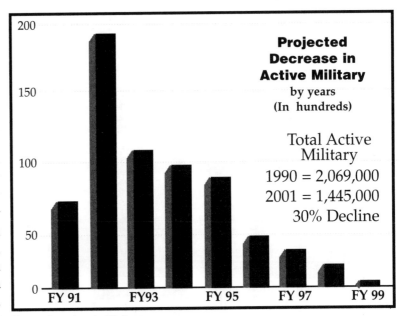

Source: Department of Defense

$40 billion. From 1990 to 2000, we will have had a decrease of 30 percent in the number of active military personnel.

Seventy-nine military bases are scheduled to close and another 26 bases are scheduled for scaling down. The Star Wars defense plan was abandoned by the Defense Department in order to reduce the amount of spending.

Because Republicans have felt that defense spending was cut too much in the early '90s, the Republican Contract with America and the House budget bill both contain measures which would increase defense spending over the next seven years.

Democrats argue that we should continue cutting the Defense Department, citing that the U.S. pays more in defense spending per capita than any other nation on earth. Democrats argue that the United States should force Western Europe and Japan to cough up more money in defending themselves and in participating in U.N. peacekeeping forces.

Democrats argue that there is less threat for America abroad now that we have won the cold war and cite statistics such as that terrorist incidents in the U.S. have dropped over the past several years.

Many, however, argue that the dangers to America are greater than ever, saying that the cold war provided a certain stability. Now they argue that conflicts arising from nationalism are arising all over the globe. In addition, leaders of Third World countries are gaining power through their purchase of high tech weapons. Ironically, these Third Word leaders get the majority of their weapons from the United States and Western Europe.

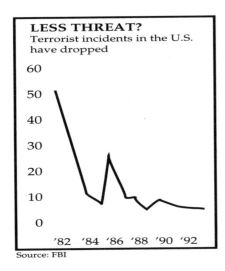

Source: FBI

39

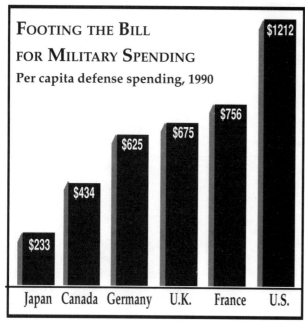

FOOTING THE BILL
FOR MILITARY SPENDING
Per capita defense spending, 1990

$233	$434	$625	$675	$756	$1212
Japan	Canada	Germany	U.K.	France	U.S.

Source: Department of Defense

Foreign Aid

In fiscal year 1995, America spent $18 billion on its foreign aid program. While that is less than 1 percent of our entire budget, foreign aid has been a hot topic politically. Many argue that our foreign aid does little if anything to help the countries that it goes to. Furthermore, many argue that the nations that we send foreign assistance are often repressive governments that are also likely to waste our money.

President Clinton argues that we should restructure our foreign aid program, but that the new Republican proposals to cut aid is reactionary. He states: "I believe these bills threaten our ability to preserve America's global leadership and to safeguard the security and prosperity of the American people in the post–cold war world."

Under the new House bill, the U.S. agency for international development, which oversees much of the foreign aid budget, would be abolished.

Presently foreign aid is given to serve three basic goals:

1. To provide humanitarian aid where needed
2. To help poor countries' economies grow
3. To improve U.S. security interests abroad

Unfortunately, many studies now show that these goals have not been achieved. One study by the Heritage Foundation showed that our top ten aid recipients have economies that are mostly not free. Furthermore, in their index of the 21 worst rated countries, all but six received U.S. foreign aid this year and last.

Additionally, many argue that the countries to which the U.S. gives money are not even friendly to U.S. interests. All but one of the top ten recipients of U.S. money took sides against the U.S. most of the time in United Nations initiatives in 1994. The exception was Israel, which cast its vote 95 percent of the time with the U.S. Egypt, which gets $2 billion in annual aid, cast votes against the U.S. two-thirds of the time. India voted against the U.S. 84 percent of the time while taking $155 million of U.S. taxpayer money. "That's as often as Cuba," noted Heritage's Johnson, author of the report.

Also, many argue that our humanitarian aid often produces the wrong consequences. For instance, the large Food for Peace program, which costs about $1 billion per year, does more harm than good to countries getting food aid, critics say. They argue that dump-

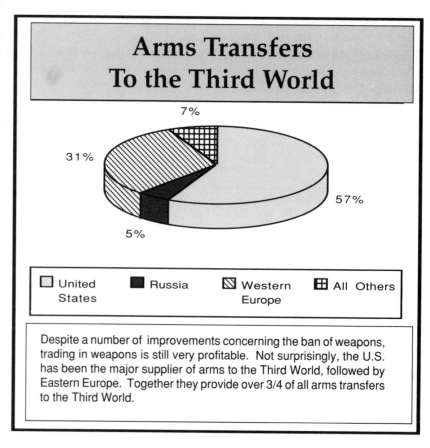

Arms Transfers
To the Third World

7%

31%

57%

5%

☐ United States ■ Russia ▨ Western Europe ⊞ All Others

Despite a number of improvements concerning the ban of weapons, trading in weapons is still very profitable. Not surprisingly, the U.S. has been the major supplier of arms to the Third World, followed by Eastern Europe. Together they provide over 3/4 of all arms transfers to the Third World.

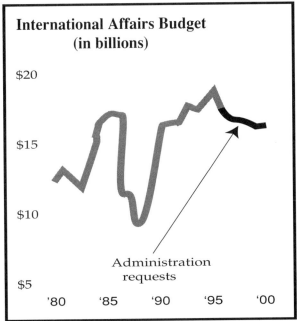

International Affairs Budget
(in billions)

$20

$15

$10

Administration
requests

$5

'80   '85   '90   '95   '00

Source: Office of Management and Budget

ing U.S. food into other countries may hurt the local farm economy.

In defense of our foreign assistance program, it can be argued that some nations to whom we have given money have succeeded. South Korea once received U.S. foreign aid and now itself sends some $100 million to poor countries. Aid chief Atwood states that the $14.8 billion in U.S. exports to South Korea in 1993 was more than all the U.S. aid sent there in the 1960s and 1970s.

Despite some successes like South Korea the foreign assistance program is likely to face cutbacks.

International Trade

Growing Interdependence

Over the past several decades, the world has become interdependent economically. Between 1965 and 1990, inflation-adjusted merchandise exports grew by 439 percent, while world production rose 136 percent. As trade becomes more important to economies, nations try to promote free trade by encouraging the people they trade with most to lower tariffs (taxes on foreign goods).

The past several years have seen the emergence of various trade organizations, including WTO, the World Trade Organization (formerly GATT— General Agreements on Trade and Tariffs), as well as organizations that create free trade zones among nations, such as in Europe (the EU), in North America (NAFTA), in South

America (Mercosur and the Andean Pact), and also in Asia (APEC).

There is talk now of a TAFTA, a trans-Atlantic free trade area uniting the three big countries of North America and the fifteen in the European union and creating a free trade zone of 750 million people with a gross regional economy of over $15 trillion. TAFTA is only an idea now, but it is being embraced by several different countries. Canada first suggested it, and Newt Gingrich wants it pursued. Both Germany and Britain have been intrigued with such an idea.

In addition, President Clinton and fourteen other national leaders in the Asia-Pacific economic cooperation forum committed themselves to complete free trade and investment by year 2020.

Just a month after that announcement, every head of government in the Americas, except Fidel Castro, was signing up for free trade from Alaska to Cape Horn by 2005. Indeed, everywhere you look, countries seem to be embracing the idea of free trade.

As we have experienced ourselves with NAFTA, the creation of free trade zones is not always an easy adjustment for countries to make. In creating free trade zones, countries often lose industries to other nations and have to rebuild their economic structure. In addition, we find that in free trade zones, nations' currencies are tied together. Not only can we look to the example of the EU for this, but also to the United States' own experience with Mexico.

When the Mexican peso began to fall in 1994 and 1995, the American dollar began to fall with it. This was because America had invested so greatly in Mexico; thus people felt devaluation with the dollar went hand-in-hand with the devaluation of the peso.

So, while free trade can be a very beneficial thing by creating specialization and greater efficiency, it also requires nations to be more interdependent — to suffer and to prosper together.

The American Agenda

Bill Clinton appointed Ron Brown as the Secretary of Commerce. During his time as Secretary, Ron Brown has done something that Commerce secretaries have never done: He has created a national export strategy which has won America export contracts worth $19.5 billion, preserving nearly 300,000 American jobs.

Ron Brown has led business missions to emerging markets such as China, Latin America, India, Turkey, and South Korea. During these missions, he has been able to negotiate to allow American businesses to export

41

to these and other countries. To his credit, America has won a $6 billion Saudi Arabia aircraft contract for Boeing, as well as helping the Raytheon Corporation receive a $1.5 billion contract for an environmental monitoring project in Brazil.

The Commerce Department has also pursued a program called ATP, Advanced Technology Program, which is a government joint investment project with private companies in what the Commerce Department calls "precompetitive technologies," or efforts that would be the basis of entire industries in the future, but are now deemed too risky for private capital. Spending on these precompetitive technologies has shot up from $68 million in 1993 to $431 million in 1995, and is projected to reach almost $750 million by 1997. While some argue that financing such projects is a wise idea, many Republicans argue that ATP is high-tech pork.

The administration has both headed and agreed to the beginnings of joining various free trade organizations as well as petitioning for U.S. export contracts abroad. The administration says that it is focused on creating markets for America because over the past seven years the export of goods and services accounted for one-third of U.S. economic growth.

The Clinton administration has made a commitment to opening up what it has identified as the twelve big emerging markets, or BEMs. By the year 2000, the Commerce Department estimates that the U.S. will export to BEMs—including China, India, and Brazil— over $200 billion, about as much as total U.S. exports to Europe and Japan combined.

Part of the idea is to attack trade barriers in BEMs before they become intractable as has happened in Japan. Some of the Japanese-American trends are already evident. China's ballooning trade surplus with the U.S. has already reached $29.5 billion in 1994, and is increasing at a rapid rate.

U.S.-Japanese Trade

Narrowly missing a crisis which threatened to unleash a trade war, the United States and Japan came to an agreement in July 1995 on their trade negotiations. Japan pledged to ease regulations that shut out U.S. replacement auto parts. According to the White House, Japan will also step up its purchases of made-in-the-USA car parts by some $9 billion over three years and increase the number of dealerships in Japan that sell U.S. cars, to 200 next year and 1,000 by the decade's end.

Critics of the trade agreements argue that this new accord will not put a dent in America's chronic trade deficit with Japan, which reached $66 billion in 1994, and still seems to be growing. In addition, many argue that the wording of the trade agreement is vague enough for Japan to slip out of its commitments. The plan also offers no specific enforcement mechanism, and thus there would be no repercussions if Japan chose not to follow the trade agreement.

Regardless of this trade agreement, the U.S. says it is still committed to breaking into Japanese markets. Secretary of Commerce Ron Brown said, "We're determined that the system has to change. Japan has been the single greatest beneficiary of free trade and open markets, yet Japan remains the single most closed economy of any industrialized country."

U.S. - Mexico Trade

In late 1994, Mexico experienced financial instability which led to a sharp devaluation of the peso. In an attempt to stabilize the peso, the U.S. put together a package of loans and credits which would help stabilize the Mexican economy.

President Clinton used the exchange stabilization fund (ESF) to provide loans and credits with maturities of greater than six months to the government of Mexico and to the Bank of Mexico.

The U.S. and Mexico signed four agreements that would provide the framework under which $200 billion in support would be made available to the government of Mexico. The repayment of these loans given by the U.S. is backed by revenues from the Mexican export of crude oil and petroleum products. Since this agreement was made, the Mexican economy seems to be improving. In fact, Mexico now has both a trade and budget surplus. In addition, the peso seems to be stable.

To better its economy, Mexico has increased its taxes on consumption, not investment or personal income, and has sold off big stakes in state-owned companies in order to raise money. In addition, the Mexican government has cut its budget by 10 percent and continued to open markets to free trade.

This is not to say that the Mexican crisis is completely over. Annual inflation rates are still expected to reach 42 percent while salaries for minimum wage workers will increase only by 10 percent. Furthermore, the budget cuts and the increase in taxes, as well as the devaluation crisis, will cost nearly one-quarter of a million Mexican jobs.

Interest rates on mortgages, credit cards and car loans have also skyrocketed to nearly 90 percent. Aside from this, the Mexican crisis has also shaken other emerging markets in Latin America. Both Brazil and Argentina, for instance, have had difficulty not only with their currency but with their stock markets.

What will happen in the future in this region remains to be seen. One thing is for sure: There will be a heated political debate around any further bailout packages for this region.

Foreign Direct Investment

Last year, the U.S. took its place as the single largest destination of foreign direct investment, attracting $41 billion.

Foreign direct investment is simply the amount of money that foreigners invest in the United States either by moving corporations and industries to the U.S.

or by buying real estate and other permanent resources of the U.S.

While the U.S. is at first place this year in attracting foreign direct investment, the trend for attracting such investment is starting to move toward developing countries. These countries took $80 billion, a 40 percent share, of the estimated $205 billion world total in cross-border direct investment. This number has been rising steadily into the '90s.

Among those nations receiving the most direct investment are China, which received $30 billion in 1994; India, which received $4 billion; and Mexico, which received $8 billion. Other nations which receive a lot of direct investment include South Korea, Kenya, and Singapore.

The best return on foreign equity comes from East Asia, followed by Africa. In last place for 1995 is Latin America.

Trade with the U.S.
(In millions of dollars)

Country	Trade Balance		Exports		Imports	
Japan	#1	-$59,354.9	#2	$47,891.5	#2	$107,246.4
China	#2	-$22,777.1	#13	$8,762.8	#4	$31,539.9
Canada	#3	-$10,772.1	#1	$100,444.3	#1	$111,216.4
Germany	#4	-$9,629.9	#5	$18,932.2	#5	$28,562.1
Taiwan	#5	-$8,933.7	#6	$16,167.8	#6	$25,100.5
Italy	#6	-$6,778.8	#17	$6,436.8	#10	$13,215.6
Thailand	#7	-$4,775.4	#24	$3.766.2	#14	$8,541.5
Malasia	#8	-$4,498.6	#18	$6,064.4	#12	$10,563.0
Nigeria	#9	-$4,406.7	#52	$894.7	#21	$5,301.4
Venezuela	#10	-$3,549.7	#20	$4,590.2	#15	$8,139.8
TOTALS [1]	$115,568.4		$465,091.0		$580,659.4	

Source: Office of Trade & Economic Analysis, U. S. Department of Commerce

[1] Includes trade with all nations—not just for those listed.

Environment

Global Warming and the Depletion of Ozone

Scientists believe that at the current rate, the earth is likely to warm by as much as 3° to 5°F over the next 50 years. This warming could set off a chain of events beginning with the melting of the polar ice caps, a rise in the sea level, flooding, and the eventual destruction of much coastal land.

Global warming is occurring because sunlight is trapped inside the earth's atmosphere by toxic gases that emanate from our industries, cars, and other man-made products. This is most commonly known as the greenhouse effect.

Greenhouse gases include chlorfluorocarbons (CFCs), methane, and nitrous oxide. The worst gases are the CFCs because they also destroy the ozone layer, which protects the earth from the sun's ultra-violet rays.

In this decade, delegates from 87 nations met in Copenhagen and together they agreed to accelerate the schedules for phasing out chemicals that damage the earth's ozone layer. Under the agreement, some chemicals would be regulated for the first time. Chloraphorbins, the chemicals thought to be the most harmful to the ozone, will be phased out by 1996. CFCs have been traditionally used in air-conditioning, cleaning, insulation, and as aerosol propellants.

The United Nations World Meteorological Organization reported discovering an ozone hole which cov-ers 3.86 million square miles—an area about the size of Europe. This hole has formed over the Antarctic.

Their figures show that in the southern hemisphere, ozone levels declined 10 percent in August from the previous year's levels. These figures, they say, support arguments for reduction in emission of ozone-destroying chemicals. The ozone layer absorbs and blocks most ultraviolet rays from the sun. Any sustained increase in that radiation coming to earth, scientists say, will lead to an increase of cancer in humans and animals, and a reduction in crop yields. The organization also says that this large ozone hole could move positions over time, perhaps reaching the southern tip of South America.

In Europe and North American, ozone has declined by 10 percent since the late 1950's, which means about 15 percent more radiation for the earth's surface. The latest findings indicate that despite actions by governments to reduce dangerous emissions, the situation for the environment will get worse before it gets better.

Deforestation and Loss of Biodiversity

The great majority of deforestation today occurs in the tropical rain forests located in Central and South America, equatorial Africa, Southeast Asia, and Northeastern Australia. It is estimated that the world may be losing more than 49 million acres of tropical rainforest each year.

With the loss of forest comes the loss of biodiversity. In a four-mile radius, a typical patch of rain forest contains 750 species of trees, 750 species of other plants, 125 species of mammals, 400 species of birds, 100 species of reptiles, and 60 species of amphibians. The destruction of all of this life has dire consequences for the human race. For example, of the 3,000 plant species that help fight cancer, 70 percent are located in the rain forest.

Destruction of Wetlands

Wetlands regulate water flows by storing water and buffering the effects of storms, purifying and filtering water, and providing a habitat for a wide variety of plants and animals.

Over the past several decades, though, wetlands have been drained, cleared, exploited, and built on. It is estimated that America has lost more than half of its original wetlands. This loss has resulted in the pollution of fresh water, loss of species, and erosion of land.

Risks According to the Environmental Protection Agency

High Risk	Habitat Destruction Global Warming Ozone Layer Depletion Species Extinction Biological Diversity
Medium Risk	Pesticides Surface Water Pollution Air Pollution
Low Risk	Oil Spills Radioactive Materials Ground Water Pollution

Political State of the Nation

Republicans: Promises and Results

In 1995, most of the Republicans running for the House of Representatives under the leadership of Newt Gingrich signed their names to a plan entitled the "Republican Contract with America." This plan promised that, if elected, these lawmakers would attempt to propose various legislation. Some of this legislation they promised to enact within the first 100 days of the Congressional session. Other legislation they promised to propose throughout their terms. Following is a summary of their plan and a report card for how they have done.

From the Contract...

On the first day of the 104th Congress, the new Republican majority will immediately pass the following major reforms aimed at restoring the faith and trust of the American people in their government:

FIRST, require all laws that apply to the rest of the country also apply equally to the Congress;

SECOND, select a major, independent auditing firm to conduct a comprehensive audit of Congress for waste, fraud or abuse;

THIRD, cut the number of House committees and cut committee staff by one-third;

FOURTH, limit the terms of all committee chairs;

FIFTH, ban the casting of proxy votes in committee;

SIXTH, require committee meetings to be open to the public;

SEVENTH, require a three-fifths majority vote to pass a tax increase;

EIGHTH, guarantee an honest accounting of our Federal Budget by implementing zero base-line budgeting.

Thereafter, within the first 100 days of the 104th Congress, we shall bring to the House floor the following bills:

1. Fiscal Responsibility Act: A balanced budget/tax limitation amendment and a legislative line-item veto to restore fiscal responsibility to an out-of-control Congress requiring them to live under the same budget constraints as families and businesses.

2. Taking Back Our Streets Act: An anti-crime package including stronger truth-in-sentencing, "good faith" exclusionary rule exemptions, effective death penalty provisions, and cuts in social spending from this summer's crime bill to fund prison construction and additional law enforcement.

3. Personal Responsibility Act: Discourage illegitimacy and teen pregnancy by prohibiting welfare to minor mothers and denying increased AFDC for additional children while on welfare, cut spending for welfare programs, and enact a tough two-years-and-out provision with work requirements to promote individual responsibility.

4. Family Reinforcement Act: Child support enforcement, tax incentives for adoption, strengthening rights of parents in their children's education, stronger child pornography laws, and an elderly dependent care tax credit to reinforce the central role of families in American society.

5. American Dream Restoration Act: A $500 per child tax credit, begin repeal of the marriage tax penalty, and creation of American Dream Savings Accounts to provide middle class tax relief.

6. National Security Restoration Act: No U.S. troops under U.N. command and restoration of the essential parts of our national security funding to strengthen our national defense and maintain our credibility around the world.

7. Senior Citizens Fairness Act: Raise the Social Security earnings limit which currently forces seniors out of the work force, repeal the 1993 tax hikes on Social Security benefits, and provide tax incentives for private long-term care insurance to let older Americans keep more of what they have earned over the years.

8. Job Creation and Wage Enhancement Act: Small business incentives, capital gains cut and indexation, neutral cost recovery, risk assessment / cost-benefit analysis, strengthening the Regulatory Flexibility Act and unfunded mandate reform to create jobs and raise worker wages.

9. Common Sense Legal Reform Act: Loser pays laws, reasonable limits on punitive damages and reform of product liability laws to stem the endless tide of litigation.

10. Citizen Legislature Act: A first-ever vote on term limits to replace career politicians with citizen legislators.

Further, we will instruct the House Budget Committee to report to the floor and we will work to enact additional budget savings, beyond the budget cuts specifically included in the legislation described above, to ensure that the federal budget deficit will be less than it would have been without the enactment of these bills.

Respecting the judgment of our fellow citizens as we seek their mandate for reform, we hereby pledge our names to this Contract with America.

Results

The Senate has approved and President Clinton has signed just two of the contract's dozen or so bills—requiring Congress to obey private-sector employment laws and restricting its power to mandate state or local programs without paying for them.

The line item veto, letting presidents erase individual items in spending bills, also cleared the Senate but its version differs so dramatically from the plan that the two chambers are struggling for a compromise. Clinton supports both.

Most House-passed bills from the GOP contract face Senate battles. One of its major provisions—the balanced budget amendment—has already been narrowly defeated in the Senate.

Most bills from the contract are in Senate committees. Hearings have been held on some, but few appear close to votes. Traditionally, the Senate postpones the toughest bills.

In late 1995, the Republicans have led debate and reform on a variety of different programs. The drive toward federalism, or turning over monies and power to state and local governments, seems to be directing this new legislation. Reform in Medicaid, welfare, and education is calling for giving block grants to states to deal with these various programs.

Republican-sponsored legislation has received opposition from the Democrats, who say that the Republicans are cutting too deep and are doing nothing more than sending national concerns to local government without the funds to solve the problems.

Republicans are pleased with their success in Congress and hope to build a strong presidential campaign on the basis of their "reform movement" in the legislature.

Democrats: Promises and Results

The Economy

President Clinton has made the first efforts to reduce the deficit. For the first time since

REPUBLICAN REPORT CARD	HOUSE	SENATE	PRES
Congressional Rule Reform			
Federal Labor Laws Applied to Congress	√	√	✍
The Fiscal Responsibility Act			
Balanced-budget constitutional amendment	√		
Presidential "line-item veto"	√	√	
The Taking Back Our Streets Act			
Crime-victim restitution	√		
Evidence-rules relaxation	√		
Death-penalty appeals curbs	√		
Block-grant anti-crime funding	√		
Speeded deportation of criminal aliens	√		
The Personal Responsibility Act			
Overhaul of welfare programs including Aid to Families with Dependent Children, child nutrition and food stamps	√		
The Family Reinforcement Act			
Tax breaks for elderly care and adoption	√	√	
Child-pornography sentencing increases	√		
The American Dream Reinforcement Act			
Per-child $500 tax credit	√		
Marriage penalty tax repeal	√		
Expansion of tax-deferred retirement savings accounts	√		
The National Security Restoration Act			
U.S. peacekeeping spending curbs	√		
Restricted U.N. command of U.S. troops	√		
Defense spending increases	X		
The Senior Citizens Fairness Act			
Social Security earnings limit reform	√		
Social Security 1993 tax-hike repeal	√		
Long-term care health insurance tax breaks	√		
The Job Creation and Wage Enhancement Act			
Small-business/depreciation tax breaks	√		
Capital-gains tax reduction	√		
Regulatory cost analysis requirements and "freeze"	√	√	
Unfunded-mandate restrictions	√		
The Common Sense Legal Reform Act			
"Loser pays" civil-suit requirements	√		✍
Punitive-damage limits	√		
Product-liability curbs	√		
The Citizen Legislature Act			
Limits on congressional terms of service	X		
√ = Legislation approved by full chamber X = Legislation defeated ✍ = Legislation signed			

Harry Truman, the deficit has been reduced for three consecutive years. Clinton has tried to scale down the government by cutting the federal work force by more than 100,000 people and by eliminating 284 federal advisory committees, and has suggested privatization of other government bodies. Overall, President Clinton has cut federal spending by about $250 billion.

In addition, the president argues that his administration helped create 6 million new jobs in the private sector through his labor policy under Secretary of Labor Robert Reich. During Clinton's administration, the U.S. has experienced the lowest combined rate of unemployment and inflation in 25 years.

Education

The president has put in place several new programs to help education. One, the National Service Act, created in September 1993, has 20,000 volunteers working in schools, hospitals, neighborhoods, and parks. Another program, called Goals 2000, the Educate America Act, was designed to allow states to develop their own plans for educational reform. In addition, the president increased Head Start funding by $760 million.

Crime

In September of 1994, Clinton signed a $30 billion Crime Bill which placed a ban on assault weapons, put 100,000 new police officers on the streets, and increased funding for certain crime prevention programs. Among these crime prevention programs are programs designed to provide after-school opportunities for children.

Health Care

Clinton revoked the Reagan/Bush restrictions on abortion counseling and RU486 imports, increased funding for WIC, and signed the Family and Medical Leave Act in February 1993. He also increased funding for breast cancer research and outpatient AIDS care.

Families and Children

Clinton expanded the earned income tax credit by $21 billion over five years, giving many families a tax cut averaging $1,400 in 1996. He also increased adoption and foster care funds by $600 million in 1994-95 and implemented a tougher child support enforcement program, which collected $9 billion in 1993, up about 12 percent from 1992.

Political Reform

Clinton signed the National Voter Registration Act in 1993, making it possible for people to register to vote when they renew or apply for drivers' licenses. He eliminated the tax deduction for lobbying expenses and imposed stricter ethics guidelines for the administration.

Free Trade

Clinton has advocated free trade, signing NAFTA into law at the end of 1993 and GATT into law at the end of 1994. Clinton also hosted the Summit of the Americas and agreed to negotiate a free trade area of the Americas by 2005. He has also pushed for trade negotiations with Japan and China.

International Relations

Clinton reached an agreement with Russia to detarget its missiles previously aimed at U.S. citizens and cities. He has worked to bring the Ukraine into the Nonproliferation Treaty, which will reduce U.S.'s and Russia's strategic nuclear weapons by over 40 percent. Clinton facilitated an agreement between Russia and the Baltics, allowing a complete withdrawal of Russian troops from Central and Eastern Europe.

Clinton helped Israel and Jordan as well as the Palestinians achieve a historic peace treaty completed in September 1995. He also sent a humanitarian mission to Rwanda and undertook, with NATO allies and the U.N., missions in Bosnia.

Working with Congress

Since Republicans have taken the majority of congressional seats, Clinton has said that he will be the safety valve in government. He feels that many of the Republicans' proposals—for instance the reform of Medicare, Medicaid, and welfare—have cut deep into the benefits that many citizens receive. He has urged Congress to slow down in its reform and in the cutting of these programs. In some cases, the president has threatened to veto certain bills which he believes are too drastic.

DEMOCRATS PROMISED	DEMOCRATS ACCOMPLISHED
• **To win passage of the tax cuts linked to education**	0
• **To develop a welfare overhaul that promotes work**	0
• **To obtain an anti-crime measure that preserves a ban on military assault style weapons**	√ **Signed Crime Bill in 1994.** • **100,000 new police** • **Ban on assault weapons**
• **To reduce the deficit**	√ **The deficit has fallen from $290 billion in 1992 to $169 billion in 1995.**
	√ **Expanded Earned Income Tax Credit.**
• **To cut taxes**	√ **Established National Performance Review.** • **Federal bureaucracy positions lessened by 102,000** • **Eliminate agencies and programs by shifting activities to states, localities, or the private sector**
• **To reinvent government**	
• **To raise the living standards of middle-income Americans**	√ **Middle-Class Bill of Rights** • **$500/child-under-13 tax credit** • **Expanded eligibility for IRA contribution** • **Tax deduction for college, university, or vocational educational cost** • **G.I. Bill for America's Workers.** • **"Skill Grants" for low-income job training**

Federal Budget Deficits
1964-2000 in Billions of Dollars

Johnson (D)	Nixon (R)	Ford (R)	Carter	Reagan (R)	Bush (R)	Clinton (D)	Projected

64 65 66 67 68 69 70 71 72 73 74 75 76 77 78 79 80 81 82 83 84 85 86 87 88 89 90 91 92 93 94 95 96 97 98 99 2000

-1.4 -3.7 -8.6 -25.2   3.2 -2.8   23.0 -23.4 -14.9 -6.1

-53.2 -73.7 -537 -59.2   40.7   -73.8 -79.0

-128.4

-149.8 -155.2 -152.5

-185.4

-$200 billion

-207.8 -212.3 -221.2   -221.4   -203.2 -192.5 -196.7 -213.1   -196.4 -197.4 194.4

-255.1

-269.2

-$300 billion   -290.4

Source: based on A Citizen's Guide to the Budget. Budget of the United States Government Fiscal Year 1996

Presidential Candidates–1996

Lamar Alexander

Tennessee's Governor Lamar Alexander began his political career in the 1960s when he worked on Howard Baker Jr.'s campaign for the Senate. In 1969, Alexander went to work for President Richard Nixon's administration as an executive assistant to Bryce Harlow in the White House's Congressional Liaison Office. In 1970, he helped run the victorious gubernatorial campaign of Tennessee Republican Winfield Dunn, and in 1978 he ran for and won the governor's office himself. His campaign was best known for his 1,000 mile walk across Tennessee during which he stayed in the homes of people across the state. Despite having a Democratic-controlled legislature in Tennessee, Alexander was able to create consensus and together they passed many legislative reforms.

In 1986, Alexander left the governor's mansion and became president of the University of Tennessee. In 1991, he became U.S. Education Secretary under President Bush. Alexander's campaign for the presidency has focused in part on education. Alexander said he would like to abolish the U.S. Education Department. Under his plan, the majority of money for elementary and secondary education would be sent back to the states as a block grant while other federal departments would handle duties such as student loans and antidiscrimination efforts.

Alexander has said many times that he wants to put more power and decisions into the hands of state and local officials. He says he would start by sending approximately $2 billion worth of federal programs including welfare and Medicaid to the states, as well as most job training programs and law enforcement duties. Alexander has traditionally been a moderate conservative. For instance in the area of abortion, he states that the federal government should "not subsidize it, encourage it, or prohibit it."

Patrick Buchanan

Patrick Buchanan, who ran for president in 1992, admits that his candidacy is a "long, long shot." Unlike many of the other candidates, he does not seem focused on winning the nomination so much as achieving some of his other political goals. He says that his aim is to create a "winning Republican coalition" by combining social and religious conservatives with economic populace who feel threatened by immigrants and international trade.

Buchanan is important in the 1996 elections because of his leadership of the Christian coalition and the Republican right. As the leader of this contingent, he will be an important political player. The religious conservatives are estimated to account for 40 percent of the GOP's primary electorate. Among the issues that Buchanan is concerned with are abortion, school prayer, immigration, and affirmative action. While Buchanan has never held elected office, he can and does attract voters with his purity, commitment, and intensity.

Bill Clinton

Elected in 1992, Bill Clinton is the youngest president since John F. Kennedy and the first Democrat in 12 years. A 1973 graduate of Yale Law School, Bill Clinton began his career in politics working in the campaigns of George McGovern and Jimmy Carter. In 1976, he was elected State Attorney General in Arkansas, and two years later he was elected governor. In 1992, not a political favorite, Clinton joined the three-way race for the presidency with George Bush and Ross Perot. Clinton garnered 366 of the 538 electoral votes despite winning only 43 percent of the popular vote.

While in office, Clinton has signed many pieces of legislation into law. Among them, he signed the Family Leave Bill, lifted restrictions on abortion counseling at federally funded clinics, and supported the UN-sanctioned Biodiversity Treaty. He laid the groundwork for the North American Free Trade Agreement (NAFTA) which started groundroads on opening trade with other nations in Latin America, Europe, and Asia. Under his supervision, Secretary of State Warren Christopher negotiated a historic peace treaty between Israel and the PLO which recognized Palestine's self-rule in Gaza, helping the Middle East resolve some of their conflicts. Clinton also encouraged the passing of the Crime Bill which placed bans on many assault weapons. Clinton, however, was not able to pass one of his major campaign promises—health care. His plan, which would have guaranteed health coverage to all Americans regardless of preexisting conditions, was met with criticism from all sides because of the strain which opponents said it put on private business.

In 1995, the president was faced with trying to get his legislation through a Republican-controlled Congress. The president has been negotiating with Senate Majority Leader Bob Dole and Speaker of the House Newt Gingrich in an effort to reach some compromise about issues such as welfare and Medicare reform. In the upcoming 1996 election, Bill Clinton may have to face leading opponents Bob Dole and Colin Powell. Polls show that Bill Clinton will likely have a close race in 1996.

Robert Dole

A front-runner in the GOP is Senate Majority Leader Bob Dole. He is by far the most experienced politician running. He is the second longest serving Republican on Capitol Hill.

Dole started his political career after graduating from law school in 1952 with a seat in the Kansas legislature. He made his first bid for the U.S. Congress in 1960 and was reelected to that seat for four terms, where he served most markedly on the Agriculture Committee. In 1968, Dole sought the seat of the retiring GOP senator, and easily defeated a former governor in the primary. Arriving in the Senate in 1969, Dole soon became an active floor debater. In January 1971, Nixon picked Dole to be chairman of the Republican National Committee. In 1976, President Gerald Ford asked Dole to be his running mate, and in 1980 Dole ran himself against Ronald Reagan for the Republican nomination for president. Losing in the primary in 1980, Dole became chairman of the Finance Committee in the Senate. Under his supervision, the Reagan tax cuts passed in 1981, along with other tax reforms that helped reduce the ballooning deficit.

Senator Dole has been busy in 1994 and 1995. With the sweeping Republican victory of the House and Senate and the emergence of the Contract with America, much new congressional legislation has been generated Medicare, welfare, crime, term limits, and balancing the budget have just been some of the issues that Senator Dole has been faced with in the past two years. As we move into the race for president in 1996, Bob Dole is still leading Republican legislation through the Senate as well as preparing for the 1996 elections.

Robert Dornan

California Representative Robert Dornan is running for the Republican nomination for president. Dornan is known for his fervent commitment to conservatism. Although Dornan is not high in the polls he said when he launched his campaign that "winning is not everything" and that he wanted to "contribute to the strength" of the country and to advancing certain issues.

Dornan is a former Air Force pilot, actor, and talk show host. He ran unsuccessfully for mayor of Los Angeles in 1973. Three years later he won a seat in Congress. In 1982, Dornan ran for the Senate, but finished fourth in the GOP primary. Dornan then moved to Orange County, where he was elected in 1984 to the House. Dornan chairs the National Security Subcommittee on Military Personnel and the Intelligence Subcommittee on Technical and Tactical Intelligence. He was a strong supporter of President Reagan's military buildup in the 1980s and the use of military force in the Persian Gulf in 1991. Dornan is a vocal opponent of abortion rights and the gay rights movement.

Malcolm "Steve" Forbes

Millionaire magazine publisher Malcolm Forbes Jr. entered his bid for the Republican nomination for president in September 1995. Forbes is the heir to his family's publishing fortune and CEO and editor of *Forbes Magazine,* a New York City–based publication. The presidency will be Forbes's first try at elected office.

Although he is little known to the public, he has been active in Republican circles nationally and in his home of New Jersey. He tends to be associated with Republicans such as Jack Kemp, who espouses economic conservatism but socially inclusive policies. The main focus of his campaign is a commitment to establish an annual federal income tax rate of 17 percent across the board with exemptions so that a family of four could file its return on a postcard and pay nothing on the first $36,000 of income. He would have no tax on Social Security, pensions, or personal savings. He wants to return the gold standard to stabilize the dollar and wants to promote an active U.S. role abroad to open trade for the U.S. He proposes cutting the federal deficit by eliminating the departments of Commerce, Energy, Education, and Housing. Forbes told the press that he is willing to spend $25 million of his own money to win the White House, but also intends to seek additional political contributions.

Phil Gramm

Senator Phil Gramm of Texas has put his bid in for the Republican nomination. Of all the candidates, he is the best financed. Phil Gramm is a native Texan who attended military school and went on to earn a doctorate in economics. Gramm began his political career as a Democrat in the House of Representatives but has since become Republican. He is now the senior senator from Texas, cultivating a national reputation as the man most likely to "buck" the Washington establishment. Gramm prides himself on being a real conservative and rallies the support of the Republican party right.

Gramm opened his career in the House in 1978 when he ran for the seat of retiring Democrat Olin Teague. In the House, he was known for shaking up the regular order of legislative proceedings and substituting his own agenda for that of the more established lawmakers. Next, Phil Gramm ran for a Senate seat. In 1983 he switched from the Democratic Party to the Republican Party and resigned his seat in the Senate; he recaptured it in a special election.

While in the Senate, he was a "budget slasher." He was concerned about the large deficits that the U.S. was running. Gramm is best known for the Gramm-Rudman-Hollings Deficit Reduction Act. More recently, he led a campaign against Clinton's health care reform in 1993 and 1994. He explained to the American people, "The Clinton plan is good old-fashioned socialized medicine—government running the health care system—they're going to reject it."

In early 1995, Gramm ranked in the polls behind Bob Dole, making him the second most popular candidate in the Republican Party.

Alan Keyes

Alan Keyes, 44, was a former Reagan administration official who now hosts a radio talk show in Maryland. He has twice been a candidate for statewide office in Maryland. Keyes was an ambassador to the U.N. Economic and Social Council from 1983 to 1985 and Assistant Secretary of State for international organizations from 1985 to 1987. Keyes is known for being extremely conservative on moral issues, such as abortion and the breakup of the family. He states that the "moral crisis in America is the fundamental issue." Keyes is essentially a commentator, like Buchanan, and has never held elective office.

Richard Lugar

In 1994, Lugar became the first Indiana senator to be re-elected to a fourth term. Lugar began running for the Senate in 1974 when he lost to Democrat Birch Bayh. Two years later, he won the seat and has been there ever since.

Richard Lugar was also mayor of Indianapolis and vice president of the National League of Cities. A Rhodes scholar, Lugar served in the Navy as a briefing officer at the Pentagon before returning home to run the family tool business. He won his first election in 1964 to the Indianapolis School Board.

During his time in the Senate, Lugar has been an independent thinker on many issues and has earned bipartisan respect by studying issues at length before taking a position. He is, however, a solid conservative who supported Bush on key votes more often than all but three other Republican senators. He is known particularly for his interest in foreign affairs. He was highly visible in 1992 and early 1993 in the debate over the U.S. involvement in former Yugoslavia. He advised both Presidents Bush and Clinton to send U.S. troops on a peacekeeping mission to this area. Lugar became President Bush's point man in Congress, strongly urging the president not only to push Saddam Hussein of Iraq back to his border, but to remove him completely.

In recent years, Lugar's main focus has been as a ranking member and now chairman of the Agriculture Panel in Washington, D.C. He has been a strong advocate of reforming the price support system and restructuring the U.S. Agriculture Department. Lugar has been a strong supporter of environmental issues while on the Agriculture Committee.

Colin Powell

Although he has not yet declared himself as a presidential candidate, General Colin Powell Jr. appears to be beating the other presidential contenders in a number of different polls around the country. As Chairman of the Joint Chiefs of Staff from 1989 to 1993, Powell was the nation's top uniformed officer. During his time in the U.S. Army, Powell served in Vietnam and Korea, and became a war hero in the Persian Gulf War.

Aside from being urged to run for the presidency, Powell is promoting his new book, *My American Journey,* in which he talks about his upbringing, his choice to enter the military, and his subsequent career in government and the military.

Powell has served in the Army for more than 30 years, has worked in the White House's Energy Department, and was National Security Adviser for the last two years of the Reagan administration. Under President Bush, he was appointed to the Joint Chiefs of Staff and served there also under Clinton until his retirement in 1993.

Because his involvement in the military precluded him from voicing his opinions on political issues, Powell's stand on current political issues is less well known than the other candidates'. In September 1995, Powell began to voice some of his opinions, beginning with an interview with Barbara Walters on ABC's "20/20." Many compare Colin Powell to Eisenhower, who took the military route to the political arena. Many also feel that Powell brings to politics a freshness, command, and strength which the other candidates do not seem to show.

Arlen Specter

Pennsylvania senator Arlen Specter prides himself on being the only GOP presidential candidate "who's willing to take on the fringe." Arlen Specter is clearly one of the most liberal Republicans. Throughout his Senate career, Specter has voted against Republican Party positions more frequently than any of his presidential rivals, particularly on social issues. He was a long-standing sponsor of the Family Medical Leave Act and backed a 1991 measure to provide up to 20 additional weeks of unemployment benefits. He has voted consistently against measures to restrict abortion or bar Medicaid funding for most abortions. In his first term, he voted against a proposed Constitutional amendment that would have allowed organized prayer in public schools.

Specter likes to compare himself to Barry Goldwater, the former senator and 1964 GOP presidential nominee. He, like Barry Goldwater, has been an economic conservative as well as one who extended his libertarian perspective to social issues, believing that the government should stay out of people's personal lives.

The son of a Russian-Jewish immigrant, Specter received an Ivy League education and made his way as a well-known prosecutor in the state of Pennsylvania. In 1964, he became an assistant counsel to the Warren Commission and authored the controversial "single bullet theory"—that President John F. Kennedy was the victim of a lone bullet and single assassin.

In 1964 Specter was a Democrat but in 1965 he switched to the Republican Party and won an election to be the Philadelphia District Attorney. In 1980, after some failed attempts at political office in his state, Arlen Specter captured a U.S. Senate seat.

Maurice Taylor Jr.

Maurice Taylor Jr. is the president and chief executive officer of Titan Tire's parent company, Titan Wheel International of Quincy, Illinois. This is a publicly owned corporation and is a leading maker of wheels for off-highway vehicles. Taylor, who has never run for public office, says that a businessman can be the best choice for president. He states that his success in business makes him the perfect choice to "manage" the executive branch. His message stresses reorganizing government and cutting bureacracy.

Other Presidential Challengers

The Libertarian Party

The Libertarian Party was founded in 1971 and is America's third largest political party with more than 100 elected party officeholders. They advocate personal and economic freedom and protest government control and interference. Libertarians say the government should do only two things: (1) provide a national defense, and (2) protect citizens' constitutional rights from state and local government violations (e.g., freedom of speech, to vote, etc.). Their platform is a strong belief in a free market, replacing government social programs (e.g., welfare, Medicaid) with private and voluntary charity institutions (e.g., United Way, Red Cross, etc.). They believe in open international borders and little military intervention abroad.

The Libertarian Party currently has four candidates running for the presidency in 1996. They are: Harry Browne, Douglas Ohman, Irwin Schiff, and Rick Tompkins. Harry Browne was born in New York City in 1933, but grew up in Los Angeles. He is an investment adviser, author, and public speaker who has appeared on numerous television programs such as the "Today" show, "Larry King Live," and other national radio and TV shows.

The Libertarian Party – Platform Summary Chart	
Abortion	Pro-choice.
Crime	Opposes gun control.
Welfare	Government deregulation, move to private charitable organizations.
Medicaid/Medicare	Government deregulation, move to private charitable organizations.
Budget Deficit	Less government spending, use gold standard in order to add value to dollar.
Taxes	Private business to replace government operations, voluntary methods of financing. government functions.
English as Primary Language	Opposes.
Prayer in Schools	Opposes.
Affirmative Action	Opposes.
Foreign Policy	Neutrality and free trade.

NOTE: The views above are a generality of the Libertarian movement summarized from materials received from the Libertarian Party headquarters; individual candidates may have slightly different or more complex platforms.

The Reform or Independent Party

The Reform Party or Independent Pary was launched by Ross Perot in September of 1995 on CNN's "Larry King Live." The party is now fighting to become a registered party in the United States so that it can nominate a presidential candidate for the upcoming 1996 election. Ross Perot launched the party, saying that Americans feel "abandoned" by the two-party system which has created much gridlock and has done "little to solve America's problems." The party is now focusing much of its effort on recruiting people to sign petitions and on registering them to vote under the new party so that it can meet its deadlines and get on the presidential ballot.

Regardless of whether or not the Reform Party is officially recognized, founders say that the party will run or help campaign for its presidential candidate. In addition, the Reform Party will actively back candidates, Republicans or Democrats, throughout the country who back the Reform Party's platform.

The Reform Party – Platform Summary Chart	
Term Limits	Limit U.S. Representatives to three terms in the House and U.S. Senators to two terms.
Campaign Reform	Shorten election cycle. Vote on weekends. Replace Electoral College with a direct vote. Prohibit announcement of exit polls until all votes are in.
Deficit	Stop off-budget accounting. Pass the Balanced Budget Amendment. Provide understandable financial reports.
Lobbying	Prohibit former elected officials or employees from taking money from foreign interests and lobbying for foreign interests. Prohibit former elected officials or federal employees from lobbying for domestic interests until five years after their employment/term has ended.
Medicare/Medicaid	Pilot tests for reform. Create a public consensus for this reform.
Taxes	Create fairer, simpler system. Require all major tax changes to be voted on by the people.

SUMMARY OF SOME PRESIDENTIAL CANDIDATE PLATFORMS

PLATFORMS

	ALEXANDER	BUCHANAN	CLINTON	DOLE	GRAMM	POWELL	LUGAR	SPECTER
Age	54	57	49	72	53	56	63	65
Party	Republican	Republican	Democrat	Republican	Republican	Not available	Republican	Republican
Abortion	Pro-life	Pro-life	Pro-choice	Pro-life	Pro-life	Pro-choice	Pro-choice	Pro-choice
Crime	Limited gun control	Opposes most gun control	Favors control on assault weapons	Favors limited gun control	Favors limited gun control	Favors control on assault weapons	Favors control on retail sales tax	Favors control on assault weapons
Welfare	Favors state control	Favors state control	Favors some federal control	Favors state control	Favors state control	Favors reform—linked to work	Favors more state control	Favors some federal control
Medicaid/ Medicare	Favors state control	Favors state control	Favors some federal control	Favors state control	Favors state control	Not available	Favors more state control	Favors some federal control
Deficit	Favors 0 deficit by 2002	Wants reduced spending/ taxes immediately	Favors 0 deficit by 2005; reduced deficit '93-'95	Favors 0 deficit by 2002	Favors 0 deficit by 2002; wrote Gramm-Rudman	Supports some congressional efforts to balance	Favors 0 deficit by 2002	Favors 0 deficit by 2002
Taxes	Favors simplification	Favors flat tax	Favors tax to spur investment	Wants to simplify, possibly flat tax	Favors flat tax, cut capital gains	Not available	Favors national retail sales tax	Wants to simplify, cut capital gains
English as Primary Language	Not available	Favors	Opposes	Favors	Favors	Not available	Not available	Favors
Prayer in School	Favors moment of silence	Favors	Opposes any	Favors moment of silence	Favors moment of silence	Favors moment of silence	Not available	Opposes any
Affirmative Action	Opposes	Opposes	Favors	Opposes	Opposes	Favors	Opposes	Not available
Foreign Policy	Limited combat under U.N. command	Favors protect-ing markets, limit military under U.N.	Favors free trade, maintain current defense spending	Favors higher defense budget, favors free trade	Opposes U.S. troops under U.N. command	Not available	Favors free trade, supports a pro-active military	Maintain current defense spending

(as of October 1995)

Financial Review

These are not the complete Consolidated Financial Reports of the U. S. Government produced by the Treasury Department. The Financial Review is only a summary of these reports. For a complete understanding, please order the actual complete reports from the Treasury Department.

Discussion and Analysis

The Financial Review is a compilation of information reported by the Treasury Department. This section will give you the government's Certified Financial Statements (CFS) for fiscal years 1992, 1993, and 1994. In this section you will find (1) the Balance Sheet, (2) the Income Statement, and (3) the Cash Flow Statement. In addition we also provide an Income Statement for the cumulative finance of state and local governments.

In looking at these documents you will notice that there are two schedules for the three main financial statements. This results from the fact that the Treasury Department changed their method of accounting from 1993 to 1994.

The 1992-1993 statements were prepared with the consulting advice of Arthur Andersen & Co., a "Big 8" accounting firm. These statements use accrual accounting, which is more representative than those compiled in the subsequent 1994 year prepared solely by the government without independent auditing opinion.

The 1993-1994 statements were prepared by the Treasury Department's internal financial managment service and were prepared on a cash basis. Therefore, they do not totally show complete finances of the federal government. For example, they do not include such items as property, plant, and equipment in the balance sheet.

We hope that the ensuing CFS will be a good source of information. We do caution that there are difficulties in the presentation of this information—Arthur Andersen & Co. provides us with the major accounting insufficiencies in federal financial reporting in their comments included in the Certified Financial Statements of the United States Government as follows:

Problems with Federal Accounting

"**Our principal finding is that the existing deficiencies, as described below, in the preparation process make it likely that the 1993 CFS is materially misstated.**

"**Accuracy and Completeness**—Treasury does not maintain or control the accounting information from which the CFS is prepared. Treasury has established a process to compile the accounting information submitted by federal entities; however, the reliability of the underlying information used to prepare the CFS rests with the individual federal entities.

"Much of this information is currently either not subject to audit or is considered unreliable as a result of audit. Additionally, because the CFS is prepared primarily from information submitted by the entities prior to audit, the CFS does not reflect certain changes arising from such audits. Treasury's process for identifying and recording changes resulting from audits of federal entities' financial statements is not adequate to detect material misstatements or omissions in the CFS. Improvements in the accuracy and completeness of information submitted by federal entities and in identifying and recording the CFS adjustments resulting from audits of this information are necessary to improve the CFS.

"**Accounting and Reporting**—A comprehensive set of accounting standards and reporting criteria do not currently exist for federal entity financial statements. The federal Accounting Standards Advisory Board is in the process of developing such standards and criteria. For example, the extent to which actual and budget data are reported and reconciled, whether long-lived assets should be capitalized and depreciated, the accounting and reporting for public domain assets, and how social security, pension plans, contingencies and unfunded liabilities should be recorded must be resolved. The development of a comprehensive set of accounting standards and reporting criteria for federal entities' financial statements and the appropriate application thereof is required to improve the CFS. Additionally, accounting standards and reporting criteria specific to the CFS governing matters such as consolidation principles and disclosure requirements are necessary.

"**Consolidation and Analysis Process**—As a result of incomplete or inaccurate reporting by federal entities, it is necessary for Treasury to make adjustments to the submitted information. However, Treasury's accumulation and analysis process, while detecting many errors, is not sufficiently comprehensive to ensure that all significant errors or omissions would be identified.

"Treasury did modify its consolidation process for the fiscal year 1994 CFS to obtain information from each entity electronically in a standardized format (i.e., each entity will transmit its information in conformity with the Standard General Ledger). Treasury is also devising reporting requirements for entities to submit necessary footnote disclosure information. These modifications should improve the consistency of information submitted to Treasury and will increase the level of detail to permit additional analysis. However, the development of a comprehensive approach for preparing the CFS is required, including matters such as (1) communication and disposition of changes resulting from audits, (2) reconciliation and elimination of intra- and inter-entity amounts, (3) adaptation of the consolidation process to respond to evolving accounting standards and reporting requirements, including a discussion of the government's performance, and (4) identification and resolution of CFS reporting entity issues, such as coordination of legal matters and contingencies with entity management and general counsel, and with the Department of Justice.

"Many of these areas are not within Treasury's direct control. Consequently, resolving issues associated with the quality of information submitted by federal entities and developing comprehensive accounting standards and a reporting framework must involve a concerted and sustained effort by the entire federal financial management community. Additionally, the recent passage of the Government Management Reform Act of 1994 increases the amount of financial information subject to audit by requiring that the 24 major executive agencies undergo agency-wide audits beginning with fiscal year 1996 and requiring that the CFS be audited beginning with fiscal year 1997. **Effective implementation of this legislation combined with a strong commitment on the part of federal entity Chief Financial Officers, etc. . . . to address these challenges is essential to improve the reliability and meaningfulness of the government's financial information.**"

Arthur Andersen LLP

Federally Reported Balance Sheets

Balance Sheet Fiscal Years 1993-1994
(In millions of dollars)

Assets:	Fiscal 1994	Fiscal 1993
Cash and Monetary Assets:		
U.S. Treasury operating cash:		
Federal reserve account	6,848	17,289
Tax and loan note accounts	29,094	35,217
Special drawing rights, total holdings	9,971	9,203
Less: Special drawing rights certificates issued to Federal Reserve Banks	(8,018)	(8,018)
Monetary assets with International Monetary Fund (IMF)	12,069	12,103
Other cash and monetary assets:		
U.S. Treasury monetary assets	415	433
Cash and other assets held outside the Treasury account	20,639	21,592r
U.S. Treasury time deposits	362	384r
Total cash and monetary assets	71,380	88,203r
Outlays:		
Loan financing accounts:		
Guaranteed loans	(9,806)	(6,320)
Direct loans	12,726	6,862
Miscellaneous asset accounts	(1,386)	(636)
Total Assets:	**72,915**	**88,109r**
Excess of Liabilities Over Assets		
Excess of liabilities over assets at beginning of fiscal year	3,219,491	2,964,535r
Add: Total deficit for fiscal year	203,615	255,306r
Subtotal	3,423,106	3,219,841r
Deduct: Other transactions not applied to surplus or deficit	715	351
Excess of liabilities over assets at close of fiscal year	3,422,391	3,219,491r
Total assets and excess of liabilities over assets	3,495,306	3,307,600r
Liabilities:		
Borrowing from the public:		
Public debt securities outstanding	4,692,752	4,411,491r
Premium and discount on public debt securities	(77,298)	(85,025)
Total public debt securities	4,615,453	4,326,466
Agency securities outstanding	28,543	24,877r
Total Federal securities	4,643,996	4,351,343r
Deduct: Net federal securities held as investments by government accounts	1,211,421	1,103,989r
Total borrowing from the public	3,432,575	3,247,354r
Accrued interest payable	43,287	43,819
Special drawing rights allocated by IMF	7,189	6,950
Deposit fund liabilities	7,316	6,249r
Miscellaneous liability accounts (checks outstanding, etc.)	4,938	3,228r
Total Liabilities:	**3,495,306**	**3,307,600r**

Note: Details may not add due to rounding.

r = revised

Author's Note: These statements are internally generated by the Treasury Department. Terminology is different. Property, plant, and equipment are not included.

Accounting methods and terminology were changed in 1993 so two reports are shown for fiscal years 1992-1994 as prepared by the Treasury Department.

Balance Sheet Fiscal Years 1992-1993
(In billions of dollars)

	Fiscal 1993	Fiscal 1992
Assets:		
Cash (Note 2)	52.5	58.8
Other monetary assets (Note 3)	136.7	135.3
Accounts receivable, net of allowances (Note 4)	66.1	65.7
Inventories (Note 5)	153.9	157.9
Loans receivable, net of allowances (Note 4)	139.5	143.0
Advances and prepayments	14.0	33.4
Property, plant, and equipment, net of accumulated depreciation (Note 6)	607.8	601.0
Deferred retirement costs	27.1	26.8
Financial assets (Note 7)	46.9	69.8
Other assets (Note 8)	117.9	152.5
Total assets:	**1362.4**	**1444.2**
Liabilities:		
Checks outstanding	25.3	27.2
Accounts payable	110.5	125.1
Interest payable	45.3	44.8
Accrued payroll and benefits	20.8	22.4
Unearned revenue (Note 9)	39.0	76.8
Debt held by the public (Note 10)	3247.2	2998.8
Pensions and actuarial liabilities (Note 11)	1602.1	1500.9
Financial liabilities (Note 12)	23.0	41.9
Other liabilities (Note 13)	125.8	99.1
Total liabilities	**5239.0**	**4937.0**
Accumulated position (Note 14)	**-3.876.6**	**-3492.8**

Note: The notes, which can be found on pp. 62-66, are an integral part of these statements. Author's Note: The accounting firm of Arthur Andersen & Co. aided in the preparation of these statements for the year ending September 30, 1993.

Federally Reported Income Statements

	Fiscal 1994	Fiscal 1993
Income Statement Fiscal Years 1993-1994 (In millions of dollars)		
Receipts:		
Individual Income Taxes	543,055	509,680
Corporation Income Taxes	140,385	117,250
Social Insurance Taxes and Contribution:		
Employment taxes and contributions (off-budget)	335,026	311,934
Employment taxes and contributions (on-budget)	93,784	85,005
Unemployment insurance	28,004	26,556
Other retirement contributions	4,661	4,805
Excise Taxes	55,225	48,057
Estate and Gift Taxes	15,225	12,577
Custom Duties	20,099	18,802
Miscellaneous Receipts	21,990	18,290r
Total Receipts	**1,257,453**	**1,153,226r**
Outlays:		
Legislative Branch	2,561	2,406
The Judiciary	2,659	2,628r
Executive Office of the President	229	194
Funds Appropriated to the President	10,511	11,526
Departments:		
Agriculture	60,753	63,112
Commerce	2,915	2,798
Defense, Military	268,635	278,586
Defense, Civil	30,407	29,266r
Education	24,699	30,290
Energy	17,840	16,801
Health & Human Services, except Social Security	310,837	282,781
Health & Human Services, Social Security	313,881	298,349
Housing and Urban Development	25,845	25,181
Interior	6,923	6,720r
Justice	10,005	10,170
Labor	37,130	44,738
State	5,718	5,385r
Transportation	37,229	34,457
Treasury	307,577	298,802r
Veterans Affairs	37,401	35,487
Environmental Protection Agency	5,855	5,930r
General Service Administration	334	743
National Aeronautics & Space Administration	13,694	14,305
Office of Personnel Management	38,596	36,794
Small Business Administration	779	785
Independent Agencies	11,525	(9,992)r
Undistributed Offsetting Receipts	(123,470)	(119,711)r
Total Outlays	**1,461,067**	**1,408,532r**
Total Deficit	**(203,615)**	**(255,306)r**
Other Transactions not applied to current year's surplus deficit		
Seigniorage (gain on coin production)	(693)	(351)
Profit on sale of gold	(21)	*
Total other transactions not applied to current year's surplus or deficit	(715)	(351)

NOTE:
Details may not add to totals due to rounding
* = less than $500,000
r = revised

Accounting methods and terminology were changed in 1993 so two reports are shown for fiscal years 1992-94 as prepared by the Treasury Department.

Income Statement Fiscal Years 1992-1993
(In billions of dollars)

Revenues	Fiscal 1993	Fiscal 1992
Levied under the Government's sovereign power:		
Individual Income Taxes	509.7	476.5
Corporate Income Taxes	117.5	100.3
Social Insurance Taxes and Contributions	428.3	413.7
Excise Taxes	48.1	45.6
Estate and Gift Taxes	12.6	11.1
Customs Duties	18.8	17.3
Miscellaneous	18.2	27.2
Total:	**1153.2**	**1091.7**
Earned through Government business-type operations:		
Sale of goods and services	92.0	94.2
Interest	10.6	11.7
Other	1.1	3.3
Total Revenues:	**1256.9**	**1200.9**
Expenses by Agency		
Legislative branch	2.3	2.6
Judicial branch	2.6	2.3
Executive branch:		
Executive Office of the President	0.2	0.2
Funds appropriated to the President	24.6	23.2
Departments:		
Agriculture	66.8	72.0
Commerce	4.1	4.5
Defense (Military)	283.1	286.7
Defense (Civil)	34.6	32.5
Education	29.8	35.2
Energy	40.9	19.9
Health & Human Services, except Social Security	266.3	232.6
Health & Human Services, Social Security	307.3	267.8
Housing & Urban Development	27.4	27.8
Interior	10.1	7.4
Justice	12.6	12.9
Labor	46.1	48.4
State	9.5	6.5
Transportation	36.5	32.5
Treasury:		
Interest on debt held by the public	205.9	210.9
Other	27.7	28.0
Veterans Affairs	79.3	86.3
Independent agencies	124.7	120.7
Total Expenses:	**1642.4**	**1560.9**
Expenses in excess of revenues	**-385.5**	**-360.0**

Federally Reported Cash Flow Statements

Statement of Sources and Applications of Funds Fiscal 1993-1994 (In millions)

	Fiscal 1994	Fiscal 1993
SOURCES		
Increases in liabilities:		
Borrowing from the public	185,221	248,594 r
Special drawing rights allocated by International		
Monetary Fund (IMF)	240	-
Deposit fund liabilities	1,067	-
Miscellaneous liabilities (checks outstanding, etc.)	1,709	1,086 r
Decreases in assets:		
U.S. Treasury operating cash:		
Federal reserve account	10,441	7,297
Tax and loan note accounts	6,123	-
Special drawing rights (SDRs):		
Total holdings	-	2,908
Funds available with IMF	35	-
Net activity, guaranteed loan financing	3,486	4,577
Other cash and monetary assets	992	1,433 r
Miscellaneous assets	749	-
Other transactions not applied to surplus or deficit	715	351
Total sources	210,778	266,245 r
APPLICATIONS		
Deficit	203,615	255,306 r
Increases in assets:		
U.S. Treasury operating cash:		
Tax and loan note accounts	-	1,014
Special drawing rights (SDRs):		
Total holdings	768	-
SDR certificates issued to Federal Reserve banks	-	2,000
Funds available with IMF	-	2,333
Net activity, direct loan financing	5,864	3,810
Miscellaneous assets	-	948
Decreases in liabilities:		
Accrued interest payable to the public	531	394
Special drawing rights allocated by IMF	-	267
Deposit fund liabilities	-	173 r
Total applications	210,778	266,245 r

Consolidated Statements of Reconciliation of Accrual Operating Results to the Budget

(In billions of dollars) Expenses in excess of revenues (current-period results on accrual basis)	Fiscal 1993	Fiscal 1992
	385.5	[1]360.0
Additions [2]:		
Changes in property and equipment	70.9	60.6
Net loan disbursements	10.8	5.2
Seigniorage	.4	.3
Total additions	82.1	66.1
Deductions [3]:		
Increase in pensions and actuarial liabilities	101.2	[1]32.9
Depreciation expense	64.1	59.9
Increase in allowances	3.1	9.2
Net accrual adjustments	44.3	33.9
Total deductions	212.7	135.9
Reported budget outlays over receipts	254.9	290.2

The accompanying notes are an integral part of these statements.

[1] Changes due to restatement of pensions and actuarial liabilities. (See Note 11.)

[2] Addition of items that are not included as expenses in the actual operating results, but are included in the budget.

[3] Deduction of items that are included as expenses in the actual operating results, but are not included in the budget.

Cash Flow Statement Fiscal Years 1992-1993
(In billions of dollars)

	Fiscal 1993	Fiscal 1992
Cash flows from operating activities:		
Expenses in excess of revenues	-385.5	-360.0
Adjustments to reconcile expenses in excess of revenues for the year to net cash used in operating activities:		
Noncash items:		
Depreciation	64.1	59.9
Increase/decrease in the value of gold	1.7	-1.6
Allowances for doubtful accounts	114.5	111.4
Additions to accounts receivable, net of collections	-58.0	-65.5
Decrease/increase in inventories	4.0	-30.1
Increase in deferred retirement costs	-.3	-1.6
Decrease in financial assets	22.9	13.3
Decrease in other assets	54.0	6.0
Decrease in checks outstanding	-1.9	-7.2
Decrease/increase in accounts payable	-14.6	25.5
Increase in interest payable	.5	1.2
Decrease/increase in accrued payroll and benefits	-1.6	4.2
Decrease/increase in unearned revenue	-37.8	10.1
Increase in pensions and actuarial liabilities	101.2	132.9[1]
Decrease in financial liabilities	-18.9	-5.5
Increase in other liabilities	26.7	39.3
Total adjustments	256.5	192.3
Net cash used in operating activities	-129.0	-167.7
Cash flows from investing activities:		
Changes in property and equipment	70.9	-60.6
Additions to gross loans receivable	-33.3	-24.9
Net repayments and reclassifications of loans receivable	-20. 1	-24.4
Net cash used in investing activities	-124.3	-109.9
Cash flows from financing activities:		
Debt issued	248.4	311.6
Net cash provided by financing activities	248.4	311.6
Net decrease/increase in cash and other monetary assets	-4.9	34.0
Cash and other monetary assets, beginning of year	194.1	160.1
Cash and other monetary assets, end of year	189 2	194.1

The accompanying notes are an integral part of these statements.

[1] *Refer to Note 11, p. 63.*

1. Summary of accounting policies

Principles of consolidation

The Consolidated Financial Statements report on the financial activity of the legislative, judicial, and executive branches of the Federal Government, and include Federal Government corporations. Under the requirements of Volume I, Treasury Financial Manual, Part 2, Chapter 4100, the legislative and judicial branches are not required to report to the Department of the Treasury. The legislative branch provides limited reports voluntarily. The Department of the Treasury estimates revenue and expense data for the judicial branch based on the "Final Monthly Treasury Statement."

All significant intragovernmental transactions were eliminated in consolidation.

Basis of accounting policies

The Secretary of the Treasury, the Director of the Office of Management and Budget (OMB), and the Comptroller General of the United States, principals of the Joint Financial Management Improvement Program (JFMIP), established the Federal Accounting Standards Advisory Board (FASAB) in October 1990. FASAB recommends accounting standards to the JFMIP principals for approval. Upon approval, they become effective on the date specified in the standards published by OMB and GAO.

In March 1993, the JFMIP principals approved the FASAB's recommended changes to interim accounting standards used in preparing financial statements for audit. Since a sufficient set of comprehensive "generally accepted accounting principles" has not been published by JFMIP principals, the revised guidance recommends a hierarchy of "other comprehensive basis of accounting" to be used for preparing Federal Agency financial statements. The hierarchy is as follows:

1. Individual standards agreed to and published by the JFMIP principals.

2. Form and Content requirements included in OMB Bulletin 94-01, dated November 16, 1993.

3. Accounting standards contained in an agency accounting policy, procedures manuals and/or related guidance as of March 29, 1991, so long as they are prevalent practices.

4. Accounting principles published by authoritative standard-setting bodies and other sources (1) in the absence of other guidance in the first three parts of this hierarchy, and (2) if the use of such accounting standards improves the meaningfulness of the financial statements.

Principal financial statements

The principal statements are unaudited and consist of the Statements of Financial Position, Operations, Cash Flows, Budget Receipts and Outlays, and Reconciliation of Accrual Operating Results to the Budget.

The Statements of Financial Position, Operations, and Cash Flows use the accrual basis of accounting in their presentation. Summary information pertaining to the budget deficit is provided in the Statements of Budget Receipts and Outlays which primarily use the cash basis of accounting. A reconciliation of the operating results on the accrual basis can be found in the Statements of Reconciliation of Accrual Basis Operating Results to the Budget.

Some cash inflows and outflows, such as debt issued, were netted due to the unavailability of certain information.

Fiscal year

The fiscal year of the U.S. Government ends on September 30.

Sources of information

The fiscal 1993 Consolidated Statements of Financial Position and the Consolidated Statements of Operations were compiled from agency and Treasury reports. The Consolidated Statements of Budget Receipts and Outlays were taken from the "Final Monthly Treasury Statement of Receipts and Outlays of the United States Government."

2. Cash

The cash reported in the financial statements represents balances from tax collections, customs duties, other revenues, public debt receipts, and various other receipts maintained in accounts at the Federal Reserve banks and the U.S. Treasury tax and loan accounts. Additionally, cash includes but is not limited to the value of outstanding checks, which are accounted for as liabilities ("outstanding checks") when issued. These checks are issued by the U.S. Treasury its agents, and have not been cleared through the Federal Reserve banks. As checks clear, the cash balance is reduced and the corresponding liability amount of "outstanding checks" is also reduced.

3. Other monetary assets

Gold

Gold is valued at market for fiscal 1993 and 1992. The market value represents the price reported for gold on the London fixing, and is based on 261,898,949,188 and 261,932,896,429 fine troy ounces as of September 30, 1993 and 1992, respectively (as reported in Treasury's general ledger). The statutory price of gold is $42.22 per troy ounce.

International Monetary Fund special drawing rights

The value is based on a weighted average of exchange rates for the currencies of selected member countries. The value of a special drawing right was $1.418 and $1.473 as of September 30, 1993, and 1992, respectively.

Cash and other assets held outside the Treasury

This item is composed of amounts held by Government collecting and disbursing officers, agencies' undeposited collections, and unconfirmed deposits, including cash transfers.

4. Accounts and loans receivable

Summary of accounts and loans receivable due from the public

The Federal Government is the Nation's largest source of credit and underwriter of risk. The Debt Collection Act of 1982 (31 U.S.C. 3719) requires agencies to prepare and transmit a report summarizing any outstanding receivables on their books.

Agencies are required to submit those reports to the OMB and the Department of the Treasury. The Federal Government uses the data in these reports to improve the quality of its debt collection methods.

In 1990, the Credit Reform Act was enacted to improve the Government's budget-

Other monetary assets as of September 30		
(In billions of dollars)	**1993**	**1992**
Gold	93.1	91.4
Cash and other assets	21.5	21.1
U.S. reserve position in IMF	12.1	9.8
Special drawing rights	9.2	12.1
Nonpurchased foreign currencies	.3	.3
Other U.S. Treasury monetary assets	.5	.6
Total other monetary assets	136.7	135.3

Inventories as of September 30		
(in billions of dollars)	**1993**	**1992**
Operating consumables	82.6	85.4
Stockpiled materials	53.5	64.1
Product components	6.9	4.7
Other	10.9	3.7
Total inventories	153.9	157.9

ing and management of credit programs. The primary focus of the Act is to provide an accurate measure of the long-term costs of both direct loans and loan guarantees, and to include these costs at the time of loan origination.

Total net accounts receivable from the public amounted to $66.1 billion in fiscal 1993, an increase of $0.4 billion from fiscal 1992. Total net loans receivable from the public amounted to $139.5 billion in fiscal 1993, a decrease of $3.5 billion from fiscal 1992.

The receivables figures on the following page differ from the fiscal 1993 "Report to Congress on Credit Management and Debt Collection" prepared by OMB.

5. Inventories

Product or service components contain amounts reported in goods-for-sale, work-in-progress, and raw materials.

Agencies use a wide variety of methods to value inventories (e.g. first-in-first-out, last-in-last-out, latest acquisition cost, and weighted or moving averages). Department of Defense (DOD) policy requires use of the latest acquisition cost method valuation.

If an item of inventory is either not reapirable or no longer applicable to DOD's needs, then the item will be valued at its anticipated net realizable cash value as either scrap or surplus material offered for sale to the public.

6. Property, plant and equipment

Property, plant and equipment includes land, buildings, structures and facilities, ships and service craft, industrial equipment in plant, and construction-in-progress. These assets include automated data processing software, assets under capital lease, and other fixed assets that have been capitalized.

Land purchased by the Federal Government is valued at historical cost. The land acquired through donation, exchange, bequest, forfeiture, or judicial process is estimated at amounts the Government would have paid if purchased at the date of acquisition.

No value has been assigned to the Outer

Continental Shelf and other offshore lands. More than 662 million acres of public domain land have been assigned a minimal value of $1 per acre, and are included in the total land amount.

Most agencies use the straight-line method of depreciation. Depreciation is estimated by Treasury for those agencies that do not report depreciation expense. Treasury estimated depreciation using the straight-line method applied to the total of reported depreciable assets. Accumulated depreciation reported by business-type operations in 1993 and 1992 was $54.4 billion and $51.8 billion on assets of $174.8 billion and $179.9 billion respectively.

The useful lives for each classification of assets are as follows:
- Buildings 50 yrs.
- Structures and facilities 21 yrs.
- Ships and service craft 13 yrs.
- Industrial equipment 13 yrs.
- All other assets 13 yrs.

The largest ownership of Federal property, plant and equipment remains within the domain of DOD, whose major equipment items and weapons systems are valued at the contract price. Fixed assets that may have been procured in different years are valued at the actual cost associated with respective year of acquisition. Real and personal property are recorded at acquisition cost. If the acquisition cost is unavailable, estimated cost at today's market price and remaining useful life are used. Capitalization policies varied, with minimum thresholds in the range of $200 to $5,000.

Property, plant and equipment		
(in billions of dollars)	**1993**	**1992**
Military equipment	642.2	595.9
Buildings & facilities	225.3	223.1
Construction	128.6	134.8
Equipment (other)	58.2	57.1
Land	16.6	14.6
Other	26.3	19.8
Subtotal	1,097.2	1,045.3
Less depreciation	489.4	444.3
Total	607.8	601.0

7. Financial assets

These are receivables and other assets (at book value less allowances) from banking assistance and failures included in the totals of the Bank Insurance Fund, the Federal Savings and Loan Insurance Corporation (FSLIC) Resolution Fund,

and the Resolution Trust Corporation (RTC).

8. Other assets

Other assets reported are summarized by agency in the table below.

Other assets as of September 30		
(In billions of dollars)	**1993**	**1992**
Defense	67.7	04.9
Funds to President	37.6	35.4
Tennessee Val. Auth.	4.5	5.0
Treasury	1.9	1.5
Energy	1.4	1.7
Agriculture	1.2	2.1
Export-Import Bank	1.0	1.0
Transportation	.2	.8
Other	2.4	.1
Total	**117.9**	**152.5**

9. Unearned revenue

Unearned revenue represents an obligation to provide goods or services for which payment has already been received. Examples of unearned revenue include unearned rent, unearned subscriptions, and advances from customers. Unearned revenue is summarized by agency in the table at right.

10. Debt held by the public

Total Federal debt held by the public amounted to $3,247.2 billion at the end of fiscal 1993, an increase of $248.4 billion from fiscal 1992.

The debt table reflects information on borrowing to finance Government operations.

This table supports the Statements of Financial Position caption, "Debt held by the public." The numbers are shown net of intragovernmental holdings and unamortized premium or discount.

Intragovernmental holdings represent that portion of the total Federal debt held as investments by Federal entities, including major trust funds.

11. Pensions and actuarial liabilities

The Federal Government administers more than 40 pension plans. The largest are administered by the Office of Personnel Management (OPM) for civilian employees and by DOD for military personnel.

These plans comprise more than 98 percent of the pension liability reported on September 30, 1993. The majority of the pension plans are defined benefit plans.

The accounting for accrued pension, retirement, disability plans, and annuities is subject to several different assumptions, definitions, and methods of calculation.

Each of the major plans is summarized in the table below and is included on the Statements of Financial Position.

Pensions and Actuarial Liabilities		
(In billions of dollars)	1993	1992
Pensions		
Civilian employees	694.8	672.0
Military personnel	530.7	515.9
Other pension plans	27.0	26.9
Actuarial liabilities:		
Veterans pensions	279.5	¹234.9
Compensation	28.3	20.7
Other benefits	41.8	30.5
Total	1,602.1	1,500.9

12. Financial Liabilities

Financial liabilities are classified as "other liabilities" on the financial reports for the funds of the Federal Deposit Insurance Corporation (FDIC) and the RTC. The funds of FDIC which have liabilities classified as financial liabilities, include the Bank Insurance Fund (BIF), the FSLIC Resolution Fund, and the Savings Association Insurance Fund (SAIF).

The balances for fiscal 1993 primarily reflect liabilities incurred from bank resolution and litigation losses. A net decrease of $19 billion during fiscal 1993 is mainly attributed to the recovery of the banking industry, the phasing out of the FSLIC Resolution Fund, and accounting changes.

As a result of the continual recovery within the banking industry during fiscal 1993, the BIF's exposure to banking assistance and failure was reduced by $10.7 billion. Since the FSLIC was the predecessor to the RTC, the FSLIC Resolution Fund will continue to experience diminishing liability until 1998. At that time, it is anticipated the FSLIC Resolution Fund's operation will be discontinued

RTC's estimated cost of unresolved or future cases was decreased by $5.2 billion, which resulted from Office of Thrift Supervision changes in estimated caseload, revisions to cost estimates for existing conservatorship, and the resolution of most cases by the end of the fiscal year. Moreover, during 1992 the RTC changed its accounting policy to account for amounts "Due to Receiverships," and the overall impact resulted in a decrease of $1.4 billion.

13. Leases

Federal agencies were first required to provide financial information about lease commitments in 1986. Agencies are attempting to accumulate the lease information required. The future aggregate minimum rental commitments for noncancelable capital and operating leases as of September 30, 1993, are detailed in the accompanying chart.

The majority of these lease commitments relate to building, equipment, and office space rental. The current portion of lease costs are included in accounts payable. The long term portion of capital leases is reported as other liabilities. Data for intragovernmental leasing transactions were not available at the time of publication.

14. Social Security

No liability for Social Security is included in the Statements of Financial Position. For purposes of disclosure, however, the total unfunded actuarial liability is determined annually. As of September 30, 1993, this liability was $7,620.8 billion. (As

Actuarial Amounts		
(In billions of dollars)	1993	1992
Actuarial expenditures	20,554.7	19,492.4
Actuarial contributions	18,691.0	17,719.8
Surplus/deficit (-)	-1,863.7	-1,772.6

of September 30, 1992, it was $7,375.9 billion.) This liability represents the present value of the projected excess of future benefit payments to those presently participating in the Social Security program over contributions still to be made by them and by their employers on their behalf.

If Social Security were accounted for as if it were a pension plan, a portion of the unfunded actuarial liability would be recognized for financial reporting purposes. Such an amount has not been presented in these financial statements.

The Congress and the trustees of the funds prepare estimates based on a different financing method they regard as more appropriate for social insurance programs.

The present values of all contribution and expenditures are computed on the basis of the economic and demographic assumptions described as "Alternative II" in the "1993 Annual Report of the Board of Trustees of the Old-Age and Survivors Insurance and Disability Insurance Trust Funds." In determining present values, contributions and expenditures are estimated for a period of 75 years into the future.

The following actuarial amounts prepared by the Social Security Administration are calculated on the assumption that future workers will be covered by the program as they enter the labor force.

Medicare has total liabilities of $3,611.8 billion for the Federal Hospital Insurance Trust Fund (Part A). This is the present value of outlays projected between October 1, 1993, and September 30, 2018. It also includes the present value of claims incurred to October 1, 1993, but unpaid as of that date and any administrative expenses related to those claims incurred by unpaid outlays.

Total liabilities of $4.0 billion for the Federal Supplementary Medical Insurance Trust Fund (Part B) is the amount of unpaid benefits as of October 1, 1993, and the related administrative expenses.

The Secretary of the Department of Health and Human Services annually determines the amount to be paid by each Supplementary Medical Insurance enrollee and by the Department of the Treasury un-

Debt Held by the Public:	Sept. 30, 1993		Sept. 30, 1992	
	Average interest rate	Total debt in billions	Average interest rate	Total debt in billions
Public debt:				
Marketable	6.374	2,904.9	6.976	2,677.5
Nonmarketable	7.736	1,503.6	8.164	1,384.3
Non-interest bearing debt		2.9		2.8
Total public debt outstanding		4,411.4		4,064.6
Plus: Premium on public debt securities		1.4		1.0
Less: Discount on public debt securities		86.4		81.0
Total public debt securities		4,326.4		3,984.6
Agency debt		24.7		18.2
Total Federal securities		4,351.1		4,002.8
Less: Federal securities as investments by Government accounts		1,103.9		1,004.0
Total Federal debt held by the public		3,247.2		2,998.8

der the authority of section 1839 of the Social Security Act.

15. Commitments and Contingencies

Commitments are long-term contracts entered into by the Federal Government, such as leases and undelivered orders, which represent obligations.

Contingencies involve uncertainty as to a possible loss to the Federal Government that will be resolved when one or more future events occur. Contingencies of the Federal government include loan and credit guarantees, insurance programs, and unadjudicated claims.

For contingencies, if amounts can be reasonably estimated and the event is probable, agencies are to report a liability on their financial statements.

OMB Bulletin 94-01, "Form and Content of Agency Financial Statements" establishes guidelines for the reporting of lease liabilities and liabilities for loan guarantees. The contingent liabilities, capital leases, and loan guarantees reported by Federal agencies on their financial statements appear in the U.S. Government statements of Financial Position under "financial liabilities" and "other liabilities."

The table to the right shows the face value of commitments and contingencies. These commitments and contingencies are reported without regard to the probability of occurrence and without deduction for existing and contingent assets that might be available to offset potential losses.

"Long-term contracts" includes both operating and capital leases. "Government loan and credit guarantees" includes guarantees in force as well as contracts to guarantee. "Insurance" includes insurance in force, contracts to insure, and indemnity agreements.

In 1990, the Bush Administration provided a range for the total cost of protecting deposits in insolvent thrift institutions at $89.0 billion to $132.0 billion in 1989 present value terms. That range was translated into nominal dollar terms of $110.0 billion to $160.0 billion. In July 1992, the Bush Administration indicated the cost could fall close to the middle of the range, or about $130.0 billion.

In 1993, the Congress approved the Resolution Trust Corporation Completion Act, which was signed into law by the President on December 17. The Act provided for the release of up to $18.3 billion of previously appropriated RTC funds that had lapsed, bringing the total funds appropriated for the resolution of failed savings and loans to $105.0 billion. The $105.0 billion includes $50.0 billion provided by the Finan-

cial Institutions Reform, Recovery and Enforcement Act of 1989 (FIRREA), $30.0 billion provided by the RTC Funding Act of 1991, and $6.7 billion provided by the RTC Refinancing, Restructuring, and Improvement Act of 1991, in addition to the $18.3 billion provided by the RTC Completion Act of 1993.

On February 24, 1994, the Clinton Administration testified before Congress that, as a result of an improved economy and lower interest rates, the $18.3 billion provided by Congress in the Completion Act should be adequate to complete RTC's part of the cleanup. This would put the final cost at the lower end of the estimated range pro-

Commitments and Contingencies

(In billions of dollars)

Commitments	1993	1992
Long-term Contracts:		
General Services Administration	9.1	7.2
Tennessee Valley Authority	3.3	6.1
U.S. Postal Service	1.8	1.5
Energy	.3	.5
Other	.6	6.0
Subtotal	*15.1*	*21.3*
Undelivered Orders, Public:		
Housing and Urban Development	190.1	191.4
Defense	38.4	69.8
Transportation	33.9	32.1
Education	22.3	24.7
Health and Human Services	15.0	34.9
Other	72.8	71.8
Subtotal	*372.5*	*424.7*
Total Commitments	**387.6**	**446.0**

Face Value of Contingencies	1993	1992
Insurance:		
FDIC Bank Insurance Fund	1,869.0	1,999.3
Pension Benefit Guaranty Corp.	950.0	950.0
FDIC Savings Association Insurance Fund	695.6	781.0
Transportation	526.4	503.4
Veterans Affairs	521.2	350.0
Federal Emergency Management Agency	256.0	233.2
National Credit Union Administration	238.7	220.4
Other	47.0	48.4
Subtotal	*5,103.9*	*15,085.7*
Government Loan and Credit Guarantees:		
Housing and Urban Development	403.9	398.2
Education	66.4	60.6
Veterans Affairs	60.6	61.1
Export-Import Bank	35.2	28.8
Small Business Administration	16.7	14.5
Agriculture	16.6	16.6
Other	20.0	20.2
Subtotal	*619.4*	*600.0*
Unadjudicated Claims:		
Transportation	32.0	32.4
Health and Human Services	17.8	9.9
Energy	7.0	7.4
Other	7.6	7.1
Subtotal	*64.4*	*56.8*
Other Contingencies:		
Energy	31.0	29.6
Housing and Urban Development	18.8	.4
Veterans Affairs	16.2	13.6
Multilateral Development Banks	6.5	6.5
Other	7.5	43.9
Subtotal	*80.0*	*94.0*
Total Contingencies	**5,867.0**	**5,836.5**

vided in 1990 by the Bush Administration. While the Clinton Administration believes current estimates are reasonable, it also recognizes that there still are too many unknown factors to provide a single estimate of the ultimate cost.

The Department of Energy recognizes a contingency, as of September 30, 1993, of $31 billion for environmental cleanup through fiscal 1997. Of that amount, $19.3 billion has been recorded as an unfunded liability in accordance with guidance issued by the General Accounting Office. The remaining $11.7 billion was appropriated for fiscal 1993 and 1994. The Department of Energy established a goal in 1989 to achieve cleanup within 30 years. The current budget estimates include future projections but do not authorize departmental budget resources beyond those already appropriated for such activities by Congress.

The Federal Government in 1993 continued to be the nation's largest source of credit and underwriter of risk. Large portions of all non-Federal credit outstanding have been assisted by Federal credit programs, government-sponsored enterprises, or deposit insurance. In particular, most credit for housing, agriculture, and education is federally guaranteed.

State and Local Government Finances and Employment

State and Local Governments – Summary of Finances: 1980 to 1992

ITEM	TOTAL (mil. dol.)				PER CAPITA [1] (dol.)			
	1980	1990	1991	1992	1980	1990	1991	1992
Revenue [2]	451,537	1,032,115	1,080,862	1,185,191	1,993	4,150	4,286	4,646
From Federal Government	83,029	136,802	154,099	179,184	367	550	611	702
Public welfare	24,921	59,961	72,661	91,788	110	241	288	360
Highways	8,980	14,368	14,561	14,800	40	58	58	58
Education	14,435	23,233	25,197	27,821	64	93	100	109
Health and hospitals	2,513	5,904	6,504	7,293	11	24	26	29
Housing and community dev.	3,905	9,655	10,233	10,876	17	39	41	43
Other and unallocable	28,275	23,683	24,943	26,606	125	95	99	104
From state and local sources	368,509	895,313	926,763	1,006,007	1,627	3,600	3,687	3,944
General, net intergovernmental	299,293	712,700	748,108	793,399	1,321	2,866	2,967	3,110
Taxes	223,463	501,619	525,355	555,610	986	2,017	2,083	2,178
Property	68,499	155,613	167,999	178,536	302	626	666	700
Sales and gross receipts	79,927	177,885	185,570	196,112	353	715	736	769
Individual income	42,080	105,640	109,341	115,170	186	425	434	452
Corporation income	13,321	23,566	22,242	23,595	59	95	88	93
Other	19,636	38,915	40,202	42,197	87	156	159	165
Charges and miscellaneous	75,830	211,081	222,753	237,789	335	849	883	932
Utility and liquor stores	25,560	58,642	60,736	62,540	113	236	241	245
Water supply system	6,766	17,674	18,034	19,147	30	71	72	75
Electric power system	11,387	29,268	30,489	30,999	50	118	121	122
Transit system	2,397	5,216	5,629	5,742	11	21	22	23
Gas supply system	1,809	3,043	3,013	3,034	8	12	12	12
Liquor stores	3,201	3,441	3,571	3,618	14	14	14	14
Insurance trust revenue [3]	43,656	123,970	117,919	150,067	193	498	468	588
Employee retirement	25,441	94,268	87,206	108,310	112	379	346	425
Unemployment compensation	13,529	18,441	18,025	27,019	60	74	71	106
Direct expenditure	432,328	972,662	1,059,805	1,146,610	1,908	3,911	4,203	4,495
By function:								
Direct general expenditure [3]	367,340	834,786	908,108	971,973	1,621	3,343	3,601	3,805
Education [3]	133,211	288,148	309,302	326,769	588	1,159	1,227	1,281
Elementary and secondary	92,930	202,009	217,643	228,917	410	812	863	897
Higher education	33,919	73,418	78,749	84,329	150	295	312	331

State and Local Governments – Summary of Finances: 1980 to 1992

ITEM	TOTAL (mil. dol.)				PER CAPITA [1] (dol.)			
	1980	1990	1991	1992	1980	1990	1991	1992
By function (cont.):								
Highways	33,311	61,057	64,937	66,477	147	245	258	261
Public welfare	45,552	110,518	130,402	154,235	201	431	517	605
Health	8,387	24,223	26,706	29,344	37	97	106	115
Hospitals	23,787	50,412	54,404	58,768	105	203	216	230
Police protection	13,494	30,577	32,772	34,545	60	123	130	135
Fire protection	5,718	13,186	13,796	14,358	25	53	55	56
Natural resources	5,509	12,330	12,575	13,049	24	50	50	51
Sanitation and sewage	13,214	28,453	31,014	32,398	58	114	123	127
Housing & community dev.	6,062	15,479	16,648	17,067	27	62	66	67
Parks and recreation	6,520	14,326	15,930	15,728	29	58	63	62
Financial administration	6,719	16,217	16,995	18,090	30	65	67	71
Interest on general debt [4]	14,747	49,739	52,234	55,255	65	200	208	217
Utility and liquor stores [4]	36,191	77,801	81,004	84,361	160	313	321	331
Water supply system	9,228	22,101	23,561	24,378	41	89	93	96
Electric power system	15,016	30,997	31,090	31,983	66	125	123	125
Transit system	7,641	18,788	20,379	21,879	34	76	81	86
Gas supply system	1,715	2,989	2,970	3,058	8	12	12	12
Liquor stores	2,591	2,926	3,005	3,063	11	12	12	12
Insurance trust expenditure [3]	28,797	63,321	74,159	90,276	127	255	294	354
Employee retirement	14,008	38,355	42,121	46,419	62	154	167	182
Unemployment compensation	12,070	16,499	22,135	32,887	53	66	88	129
By character and object:								
Current operation	307,811	700,131	762,007	823,494	1,359	2,828	3,022	3,228
Capital outlay.................................	62,894	123,069	131,650	134,521	278	495	522	527
Construction	51,492	89,114	96,654	100,533	227	358	383	394
Equipment, land and existing structures	11,402	33,955	34,996	33,988	50	137	139	133
Assistance and subsidies.................	15,222	27,227	30,456	33,320	67	109	121	130
Interest on debt (general and utility)	17,604	58,914	61,533	64,789	78	237	244	354
Insurance benefits and repayments	28,797	63,321	74,159	90,276	127	255	294	354
Expenditure for salaries and wages	*163,896*	*341,158*	*366,406*	*378,804*	*723*	*1,372*	*1,453*	*1,485*
Debt outstanding, year end	**335,603**	**860,584**	**915,711**	**970,043**	**1,481**	**3,460**	**3,631**	**3,719**
Long-term	322,456	841,278	894,019	948,710	1,423	3,383	3,545	3,458
Short-term	13,147	19,306	21,692	21,333	58	78	86	85
Issued	42,364	108,468	118,054	155,060	187	436	468	608
Retired	17,404	64,831	65,666	99,233	77	261	260	399

[1] 1980 and 1990 based on enumerated resident population as of April 1. Other years based on estimated resident population as of July 1.

[2] Aggregates exclude duplicative transactions between state and local governments; see source.

[3] Includes amounts not shown separately.

[4] Interest on utility debt included in "utility expenditure." For total interest on debt, see "Interest on debt (general and utility)."

Source: U.S. Bureau of the Census, *Historical Statistics on Governmental Finances and Employment* and *Government Finances*, series GF, No. 5, annual.

Leadership in the Capital–The Administration

President — William Jefferson Clinton
Vice President — Albert Gore, Jr.
Terms of office for president and vice president: 1/20/93 to 1/20/97*

THE CABINET
Secretary of State — Warren M. Christopher
Secretary of Treasury — Robert Rubin
Secretary of Defense — William Perry
Attorney General — Janet Reno
Secretary of Interior — Dan Glickman
Secretary of Agriculture — Henry Wallace
Secretary of Commerce — Ronald H. Brown
Secretary of Labor — Robert B. Reich
Sec. of Health and Human Services — Donna E. Shalala
Sec. of Housing & Urban Development — Henry G. Cisneros
Secretary of Transportation — Federico F. Pena
Secretary of Energy — Hazel R. O'Leary
Secretary of Education — Richard W. Riley
Secretary of Veterans Affairs — Jesse Brown

THE WHITE HOUSE STAFF
1600 Pennsylvania Avenue, NW, Washington, D.C. 20500
White House Info: 202/456-1414

Chief of Staff — Leon E. Panetta
Assts. to the President & Deputy Chiefs of Staff —
Harold Ickes and Phil Lader
Sr. Adviser to the President — George Stephanopoulos
Assistant to the President:
  Counsel to the President on Domestic Policy —
  Carol Rasco
  Public Events & Initiatives — Marcia Hale
  Science & Technology — Dr. John H. Gibbons
  Press Secretary — Mike McCurry
  Legislative Affairs — Pat Griffin
  Communications — Mark Gearan
  Economic & Domestic Affairs — Robert Rubin
  Management & Admin. — [vacant]
  Cabinet Secretary — Christine A. Varney
  National Security — W. Anthony Lake
  Staff Secretary — John Podesta
  National Service — Eli Segal
  Media Affairs — Jeff Eller
AIDS Policy Coordinator — Patricia Fleming
Executive Agencies:
  Council of Economic Advisers — Laura D'Andrea Tyson
  National Economic Council — Robert Rubin, dir.
  Central Intelligence Agency — R. James Woolsey, dir.
  Office of Nat'l. Drug Control Policy — Lee P. Brown, dir.
  Office of Management and Budget — Alice Rivlin, dir.
  U.S. Trade Representative — Michael Kantor
  Council on Environmental Quality — Ray Clark, chmn.

DEPARTMENT OF STATE (202-647-4000)
2201 C Street, NW, Washington, D.C. 20520

Secretary of State — Warren M. Christopher
Deputy Secretary — Clifton R. Wharton, Jr.
Under Secretary for Political Affairs — Arnold Kanter
Under Secretary for International Security Affairs —
Reginald Bartholomew
Under Sec. for Mgmt. — Brian Atwood
Under Secretary for Global Affairs — Timothy Wirth
Legal Advisor — Sherman M. Funk
Assistant Secretaries for:
  Administration — Patrick F. Kennedy
  African Affairs — George E. Moose
  Consular Affairs — Mary A. Ryan
  Diplomatic Security — Tony Quainton
  East Asian & Pacific Affairs — Winston Lord
  European & Business Affairs — M. T. Niles
  Human Rights/Humanitarian Affairs — John H. F. Shattuck
  Intelligence & Research — Tobi Gati
  Inter-American Affairs — Alexander Watson
  International Organization Affairs — Douglas J. Bennett, Jr.
  Legislative Affairs — Wendy R. Sherman
  Near-Eastern & South Asian Affairs — John Kelley
  Oceans, International Environmental &
  Scientific Affairs — Elinor G. Constable
  Politico-Military Affairs — Robert L. Galucci
  Public Affairs — Thomas Dinilon
  South Asian Affairs — Robin Raphel

DEPARTMENT OF THE TREASURY (202-622-2000)
1500 Pennsylvania Avenue, NW, Washington, D.C. 20220

Secretary of the Treasury — Robert Rubin

Deputy Secretary of the Treasury — Lawrence Summers
Under Secretary for Domestic Finance — Frank N. Newman
Under Secretary for Int'l. Affairs — [vacant]
General Counsel — Edward Knight
Assistant Secretaries for:
  Economic Policy — Alicia Hancock Munnell
  Enforcement — Ronald K. Noble
  International Affairs — Jeffrey Shafer
  Legislative Affairs — Mary B. Levy
  Public Affairs & Public Liaison — Jack R. DeVore
  Tax Policy — Leslie B. Samuels
Bureaus:
  Comptroller of the Currency —
  Eugene A. Ludwig
  Customs — George J. Weise, comm.
  Engraving and Printing —
  Peter H. Daley, dir.
  Federal Law Enforcement Training
  Center — Charles F. Rinkevich, dir.
  Internal Revenue Service —
  Margaret Richardson, comm.
  Mint — Philip Diehl, dir.
  Public Debt — Richard L. Gregg, comm.
  U.S. Secret Service — Guy Caputo, act. dir.

DEPARTMENT OF DEFENSE (703-545-6700)
The Pentagon, Washington, D.C. 20301

Secretary of Defense — William Perry
Under Sec. for Acquisitions — [vacant]
Under Secretary for Policy — Frank Wisner
Asst. Secretaries for:
  Policy & Plans — Graham T. Allison
  Public Affairs — Kathleen DeLaski
  Reserve Affairs — Deborah Lee
  Special Operations & Low Intensity
  Comptroller — John Hamre
General Counsel — [vacant]
Administration — Ann Reese, dir.
Chairman, Joint Chiefs of Staff —
Gen. John Shalikashvili
Secretary of the Army — Togo West
Secretary of the Navy — John Dalton
Secretary of the Air Force — Sheila Widnall

DEPARTMENT OF JUSTICE (202-514-2000)
Constitution Ave. & 10th St., NW, Washington, D.C. 20530

Attorney General — Janet Reno
Dep. Attorney General — Jamie S. Gorelick
Assoc. Attorney General — William Bryson
Solicitor General — Drew Days, III
Assistants:
  Antitrust Division — Anne Bingaman
  Civil Division — Frank Hunger
  Civil Rights Division — JoAnn Harris
  Environment & Natural Resources
  Division — Lois Schiffer
  Legal Counsel — Walter Delinger
  Legal Policy — Eleanor Acheson
  Legislative Affairs — Sheila Anthony
Federal Bureau of Investigation — Louis J. Freeh, dir.
Executive Office for Immigration Review — Jack Perkins
Bureau of Prisons — Kathleen M. Hawk, dir.
Comm. Relations Service — Jeffrey Weiss, act. dir.
Drug Enforcement Adm. — Thomas Constantine
Office of Special Counsel for Immigration — [vacant]
Executive Office for U.S. Trustees — William Baity, dir.
Executive Office for U.S. Attorneys —
Anthony C. Moscato, dir.
Immigration & Naturalization Service — Doris Meissner
Pardon Attorney — Margaret Love
U.S. Parole Commission — Edward F. Reilly, Jr., chmn.
U.S. Marshals Service — Eduardo Gonzalez, dir.
U.S. National Central Bureau of Interpol —
Shelley G. Altenstadtero, chief

DEPARTMENT OF THE INTERIOR (202-208-3171)
C St. between 18th & 19th St, NW, Washington, D.C. 20240

Secretary of the Interior — Dan Glickman
Deputy Secretary — [vacant]
Asst. Secretaries for:
Fish, Wildlife, and Parks — George T. Framton, Jr.
  Indian Affairs — Ada Deer
  Land & Minerals — Robert Armstrong
  Policy, Budget & Management — Bonnie R. Cohen
  Ter. & Int'l. Affairs — Leslie Turner

  Water & Science — Elizabeth A. Reike
Bureau of Land Management — Jim Baca, dir.
Bureau of Mines — Herman Enzer, act. dir.
Bureau of Reclamation — Daniel T.
Beard, comm.
Fish & Wildlife Service — Mollie Beattie, dir.
Geological Survey — Robert Hirsch, act. dir.
National Park Service — Roger Kennedy, dir.
Public Affairs — Kevin Sweeney, dir.
Office of Congressional and Legislative
Affairs — Stephanie Solien
Solicitor — John D. Leshy

DEPARTMENT OF AGRICULTURE (202-447-2791)
The Mall, 12th & 14th Streets, Washington, D.C. 20250

Secretary of Agriculture — Henry Wallace
Asst. Secretaries for:
  Administration — Wardell Townsend, Jr.
  Congressional Relations — Robin Rorapaugh
  Economics — Keith Collins, act.
  Food & Consumer Services — Ellen Haas
  Int'l. Affairs & Commod. Programs —
  Eugene Moos
  Marketing and Inspection Services —
  Eugene Branstool
  Natural Resources & Environment —
  James Lyons
  Science & Education — R. D. Plowman, act.
General Counsel — James Gilliland
Inspector General — Charles Gillum, act.
Public Affairs — Ali Webb
Press Secretary — [vacant]

DEPARTMENT OF COMMERCE (202-482-2000)
14th St., Constitution & E. St. NW, Washington, D. C. 20230

Secretary of Commerce — Ronald H. Brown
Chief of Staff — Robert Stein
Asst. Secretaries for:
  Export Enforcement — Douglas Lavin
  Import Administration — Susan Esserman
  Oceans & Atmosphere — Douglas K. Hall
Under Secy. for International Trade — William Reinson
Under Secy. for Econ. Affairs — Everett Ehrlich
Under Secy. for Technology — Mary Lowe Good
Nat'l. Inst. for Standards & Techn. — Arati Prabhakar, dir.
Minority Business Development Agency — Joe Lira
Public Affairs — Jill Stryker, dir.

DEPARTMENT OF LABOR (202-219-5000)
200 Constitution Avenue, NW, Washington, D. C. 20210

Secretary of Labor — Robert B. Reich
Deputy Secretary — Thomas P. Glynn
Chief of Staff — Kathryn Higgins
Asst. Secretaries for:
  Congress. & Intergovernmental Affairs — Geri Palast
  Employment & Training — Doug Ross
  Occupational Safety & Health — Joseph Dear
  Pension & Welfare Benefits — Olena Berg
  Policy — John Donahue
  Public Affairs — Anne Lewis
Solicitor of Labor — Thomas S. Williamson
Women's Bureau — Karen Nussbaum, dir.
Inspector General — Charles Master
Bureau of Labor Statistics — Katharine Abraham

DEPARTMENT OF HEALTH & HUMAN SERVICES
(202-619-0257) *200 Independence Avenue, SW,
Washington, D. C. 20201*

Secretary of HHS — Donna E. Shalala
Asst. Secretaries for:
  Children & Families — Mary Jo Bane
  Health — Philip Lee
  Legislation — Jerry D. Klepner
  Management & Budget — Kenneth Apfel
  Personnel Admin. — Thomas McFee
  Planning & Evaluation — David T. Ellwood
  Public Affairs — Avis LaVelle
General Counsel — Harriet Rabb
Inspector General — June Gibbs Brown
Surgeon General — Audrey F. Manley, act.
Social Security Adm. — Shirley Sears Chater

Editor's Note: These listings are current as of October 1995.

DEPT. OF HOUSING & URBAN DEVELOPMENT (202-708-1422) *451 7th Street, SW, Washington, D. C. 20410*

Sec. of Housing & Urban Development —Henry G. Cisneros
Deputy Secretary — Terrence Duvernay
Asst. Secretaries for:
 Community Planning & Development —
  Andrew Cuomo
 Fair Housing & Equal Opportunity —
  [vacant]
 Field Management —[vacant]
 Housing & Federal Housing Commissioner —
  Nicolas P. Retsinas
 Labor Relations — Joseph A. Scudero
 Congressional & Intergovernmental Relations —
  William J. Gilmartin
 Policy Dvlpt. & Research — Michael Stegman
 Public Affairs — Jean Nolan
 Public & Indian Housing — Joseph Shuldiner
General Counsel — Nelson Diaz
Inspector General — Susan Gaffney

DEPARTMENT OF TRANSPORTATION (202-366-4000) *400 7th Street, SW, Washington, D. C. 20590*

Secretary of Transportation — Federico F. Pena
Deputy Secretary — Mortimer L. Downey
Asst. Secretaries for:
 Administration — Jon H. Seymour
 Budget & Programs — Louise Stroll
 Public Affairs — Richard I. Mintz
U. S. Coast Guard Commandant — Adm. Robert Kramek, USCG
Federal Aviation Admin. — David Hinson
Federal Highway Admin. — Rodney Slater
Federal Railroad Admin. — Jolene Molitoris
Maritime Admin. — Albert Herberger
Federal Transit — Gordon J. Linton
St. Lawrence Seaway Dvlpt. Corp. — Stan E. Parris

DEPARTMENT OF ENERGY (202-586-5000) *1000 Independence Avenue, SW, Washington, D. C. 20585*

Secretary of Energy — Hazel R. O'Leary
Deputy Secretary — William H. White
General Counsel — Robert Nordhaus
Inspector General — John C. Layton
Asst. Secretaries for:
 Congressional & Intergovernmental Affairs —
  William Taylor
 Defense Programs — Victor Reis
 Domestic & Int'l. Energy Policy — Susan Tierney
 Environment, Safety & Health — Tara Jeanne O'Toole
Energy Information Adm. — Jay Hakes, adm.
Econ. Regulatory Adm. — Jay Thompson, act. adm.
Fed. Energy Regulatory Comm. — Elizabeth Moler, chair.
Energy Research — Martha Krebs

DEPARTMENT OF EDUCATION (202-708-5366) *400 Maryland Avenue, SW, Washington, D. C. 20202*

Secretary of Education — Richard W. Riley
Under Secretary — Marshall S. Smith
Deputy Secretary — Madeline Kumin
Chief of Staff — Bill Webster
Inspector General — James B. Thomas, Jr.
General Counsel — Judith Winston
Asst. Secretaries for:
 Adult & Vocational Education — Augusta Kappner
 Civil Rights — Norman V. Cantu
 Educational Research & Improvement —
  Porter Robinson
 Elementary & Secondary Education —
  Thomas W. Payzant
 Legislation & Congressional Affairs — Kay Casstevens
 Postsecondary Education — David Longanecker
 Special Education & Rehabilitative Svcs. —
  Judith Heumann

DEPARTMENT OF VETERANS AFFAIRS (202-273-4900) *810 Vermont Avenue, NW, Washington, D.C. 20420*
Secretary of Veterans Affairs — Jesse Brown
Deputy — Hershel W. Gober
Asst. Secretaries for:
 Acquisition & Facilities — Gary Krump, act.
 Congressional Affairs — Edward P. Scott
 Finance & Information Resources Mgmt. —
  D. Mark Catlett
 Human Resources & Adm. — Eugene Brickhouse
 Policy & Planning — Victor P. Raymond
 Public & Intergovernmental Affairs — Kathy E. Jurado
Inspector General — Stephen Trodden
National Cemetary System — Jerry W. Bowen, dir.
General Counsel — Mary Lou Keener
Board of Veterans Appeals — Charles L. Cragin, chmn.

* No person may be elected president of the United States
 for more than two, 4-year terms

Editor's Note:

As a citizen of the United States, you should always feel free to write or call any member of the government, especially those who represent you directly in Congress.

This is why we have provided you with the names and addresses of the administration and all members of the U.S. Congress.

Your representatives and others serving in the government want to hear from you and learn how you feel about issues that face this nation and your particular area of the country.

One letter or call can make a difference in the way a U.S. Senator or U.S. Representative votes in Washington, D.C.

Your representatives in Washington, D.C., also have offices in their states. You are encouraged to visit your representatives in person with your questions and comments.

Public and school libraries have references explaining how to effectively communicate with our leaders.

The 104th Congress

ALABAMA

Senators
Senator Howell T. Heflin (D)
728 Hart Senate
Office Building
Washington, D.C. 20510
Phone: 202-224-4124
FAX: 202-224-3149

Senator Richard C. Shelby (R)
509 Hart Senate
Office Building
Washington, D.C. 20510
Phone: 202-224-5744
FAX: 202-224-3416

Representatives
Rep. Sonny Callahan (R)
(First District)
2418 Rayburn House
Office Building
Washington, D.C. 20515
Phone: 202-225-4931
FAX: 202-225-0562

Rep. Terry Everett (R)
(Second District)
208 Cannon House
Office Building
Washington, D.C. 20515
Phone: 202-225-2901
FAX: (Unlisted)

Rep. Glen Browder (D)
(Third District)
1221 Longworth House
Office Building
Washington, D.C. 20515
Phone: 202-225-3261
FAX: 202-225-9020

Rep. Tom Bevill (D)
(Fourth District)
2302 Rayburn House
Office Building
Washington, D.C. 20515
Phone: 202-225-4876
FAX: 202-225-1604

Rep. Robert "Bud" Cramer (D)
(Fifth District)
1318 Longworth House
Office Building
Washington, D.C. 20515
Phone: 202-225-4801
FAX: 202-225-4392

Rep. Spencer Bachus (R)
(Sixth District)
216 Cannon House
Office Building
Washington, D.C. 20515
Phone: 202-225-4921
FAX: 202-225-2082

Rep. Earl F. Hilliard (D)
(Seventh District)
1007 Longworth House
Office Building
Washington, D.C. 20515
Phone: 202-225-2665
FAX: 202-226-0772

ALASKA

Senators
Senator Ted Stevens (R)
522 Hart Senate
Office Building
Washington, D.C. 20510
Phone: 202-224-3004
FAX: 202-224-2354

Senator Frank H. Murkowski (R)
706 Hart Senate
Office Building
Washington, D.C. 20510
Phone: 202-224-6665
FAX: 202-224-5301

Representative At Large
Rep. Don Young (R)
2331 Rayburn House
Office Building
Washington, D.C. 20515
Phone: 202-225-5765
FAX: 202-225-0425

ARIZONA

Senators
Senator Jon Kyl (R)
328 Hart Senate
Office Building
Washington, D.C. 20510
Phone: 202-224-4521
FAX: 202-224-2302

Senator John S. McCain (R)
111 Russell Senate
Office Building
Washington, D.C. 20510
Phone: 202-224-2235
FAX: 202-228-2862

Representatives
Rep. Matt Salmon (R)
(First District)
1607 Longworth House
Office Building
Washington, D.C. 20515
Phone: 202-225-2635
FAX: 202-225-2607

Rep. Ed. Pastor (D)
(Second District)
408 Cannon House
Office Building
Washington, D.C. 20515
Phone: 202-225-4065
FAX: 202-225-1655

Rep. Bob Stump (R)
(Third District)
211 Cannon House
Office Building
Washington, D.C. 20515
Phone: 202-225-4576
FAX: 202-225-6328

Rep. John Shadegg (R)
(Fourth District)
2440 Rayburn House
Office Building
Washington, D.C. 20515
Phone: 202-225-3361
FAX: 202-225-1143

Rep. James Thomas Kolbe (R)
(Fifth District)
405 Cannon House
Office Building
Washington, D.C. 20515
Phone: 202-225-2542
FAX: 202-225-0378

Rep. J. D. Hayworth (R)
(Sixth District)
1024 Longworth House
Office Building
Washington, D.C. 20515
Phone: 202-225-2190
FAX: 202-225-8819

ARKANSAS

Senators
Senator Dale Bumpers (D)
229 Dirksen Senate
Office Building
Washington, D.C. 20510
Phone: 202-224-4843
FAX: 202-224-6435

Senator David H. Pryor (D)
267 Russell Senate
Office Building
Washington, D.C. 20510
Phone: 202-224-2353
FAX: 202-224-8261

Representatives
Rep. Blanche Lambert (D)
(First District)
1204 Longworth House, Office Building
Washington, D.C. 20515
Phone: 202-225-4076
FAX: 202-225-4654

Rep. Ray Thornton (D)
(Second District)
1214 Longworth House
Office Building
Washington, D.C. 20515
Phone: 202-225-2506
FAX: 202-225-9273

Rep. Tim Hutchinson (R)
(Third District)
1541 Longworth House
Office Building
Washington, D.C. 20515
Phone: 202-225-4301
FAX: 202-225-7492

Rep. Jay Dickey (R)
(Fourth District)
1338 Longworth House
Office Building
Washington, D.C. 20515
Phone: 202-225-3772
FAX: 202-225-1314

CALIFORNIA

Senators
Senator Barbara Boxer (D)
112 Hart Senate
Office Building
Washington, D.C. 20510
Phone: 202-224-3553
FAX: 202-224-6252

Senator Dianne Feinstein (D)
331 Hart Senate
Office Building
Washington, D.C. 20510
Phone: 202-224-3841
FAX: 202-224-0656

Representatives
Rep. Frank Riggs (R)
(First District)
114 Cannon House
Office Building
Washington, D.C. 20515
Phone: 202-225-3311
FAX: 202-225-7710

Rep. Wally Herger (R)
(Second District)
2433 Longworth House
Office Building
Washington, D.C. 20515
Phone: 202-225-3076
FAX: 202-225-1609

Rep. Vic Fazio (D)
(Third District)
2113 Rayburn House
Office Building
Washington, D.C. 20515
Phone: 202-225-5716
FAX: 202-225-0354

Rep. John T. Doolittle (R)
(Fourth District)
1542 Longworth House
Office Building
Washington, D.C. 20515
Phone: 202-225-2511
FAX: 202-225-5444

Rep. Robert T. Matsui (D)
(Fifth District)
2311 Rayburn House
Office Building
Washington, D.C. 20515
Phone: 202-225-7163
FAX: 202-225-0566

Rep. Lynn Woolsey (D)
(Sixth District)
439 Cannon House
Office Building
Washington, D.C. 20515
Phone: 202-225-5161
FAX: 202-225-5163

Rep. George Miller (D)
(Seventh District)
2205 Rayburn House
Office Building
Washington, D.C. 20515
Phone: 202-225-2095
FAX: 202-225-5609

Rep. Nancy Pelosi (D)
(Eighth District)
240 Cannon House Office Building
Washington, D.C. 20515
Phone: 202-225-4965
FAX: 202-225-8259

Rep. Ronald V. Dellums (D)
(Ninth District)
2108 Rayburn House
Office Building
Washington, D.C. 20515
Phone: 202-225-2661
FAX: 202-225-9817

Rep. Bill Baker (R)
(Tenth District)
1714 Longworth House
Office Building
Washington, D.C. 20515
Phone: 202-225-1880
FAX: 202-225-2150

Rep. Richard W. Pombo (R)
(Eleventh District)
1519 Longworth House
Office Building
Washington, D.C. 20515
Phone: 202-225-1947
FAX: 202-226-0861

Rep. Tom Lantos (D)
(Twelfth District)
2182 Rayburn House
Office Building
Washington, D.C. 20515
Phone: 202-225-3531
FAX: 202-225-3127

Rep. Fortney H. "Pete" Stark (D)
(Thirteenth District)
239 Cannon House Office Building
Washington, D.C. 20515
Phone: 202-225-5065
FAX: (Unlisted)

Rep. Anna G. Eshoo (D)
(Fourteenth District)
1505 Longworth House
Office Building
Washington, D.C. 20515
Phone: 202-225-8104
FAX: 202-225-8890

Rep. Norman Y. Mineta (D)
(Fifteenth District)
2221 Rayburn House, Office Building
Washington, D.C. 20515
Phone: 202-225-2631
FAX: (Unlisted)

Rep. Zoe Lofgren (D)
(Sixteenth District)
2307 Rayburn House Office Building
Washington, D.C. 20515
Phone: 220-225-3072
FAX: 202-225-9460

Rep. Sam Farr (D)
(Seventeenth District)
1216 Longworth House
Office Building
Washington, D.C. 20515
Phone: 202-225-2861
FAX: 202-225-2861

Rep. Gary Condit (D)
(Eighteenth District)
1123 Longworth House
Office Building
Washington, D.C. 20515
Phone: 202-225-6131
FAX: 202-225-0819

Rep. George Radanovich (R)
(Nineteenth District)
1226 Longworth House
Office Building
Washington, D.C. 20515
Phone: 202-225-4540
FAX: 202-225-5274

Rep. Calvin Dooley (D)
(Twentieth District)
1227 Longworth House
Office Building
Washington, D.C. 20515
Phone: 202-225-3341
FAX: 202-225-9308

Rep. William M. Thomas (R)
(Twenty-First District)
2209 Rayburn House
Office Building
Washington, D.C. 20515
Phone: 202-225-2915
FAX: 202-225-8798

Rep. Andrea Seastrand (R)
(Twenty-Second District)
113 Cannon House
Office Building
Washington, D.C. 20515
Phone: 202-225-3601
FAX: 202-226-1015

Rep. Elton William Gallegly (R)
(Twenty-Third District)
2441 Rayburn House
Office Building
Washington, D.C. 20515
Phone: 202-225-5811
FAX: 202-225-0713

Rep. Anthony C. Beilenson (D)
(Twenty-Fourth District)
2465 Rayburn House
Office Building
Washington, D.C. 20515
Phone: 202-225-5911
FAX: (Unlisted)

Rep. Howard P. "Buck" McKeon (R)
(Twenty-Fifth District)
307 Cannon House
Office Building
Washington, D.C. 20515
Phone: 202-225-1956
FAX: 202-226-0683

Rep. Howard L. Berman (D)
Twenty-Sixth District)
2201 Rayburn House
Office Building
Washington, D.C. 20515
Phone: 202-225-4695
FAX: 202-225-5279

Rep. Carlos J. Moorhead (R)
(Twenty-Seventh District)
2346 Rayburn House
Office Building
Washington, D.C. 20515
Phone: 202-225-4176
FAX: 202-226-1279

Rep. David Timothy Dreier (R)
(Twenty-Eighth District)
411 Cannon House
Office Building
Washington, D.C. 20515
Phone: 202-225-2305
FAX: 202-225-4745

Rep. Henry A. Waxman (D)
(Twenty-Ninth District)
2408 Rayburn House
Office Building
Washington, D.C. 20515
Phone: 202-225-3976
FAX: 202-225-4099

Rep. Xavier Becerra (D)
(Thirtieth District)
1710 Longworth House
Office Building
Washington, D.C. 20515
Phone: 202-225-6235
FAX: 202-225-2202

Rep. Matthew G. Martinez (D)
(Thirty-First District)
2231 Rayburn House
Office Building
Washington, D.C. 20515
Phone: 202-225-5464
FAX: 202-225-5467

Rep. Julian Carey Dixon (D)
(Thirty-Second District)
2400 Rayburn House
Office Building
Washington, D.C. 20515
Phone: 202-225-7084
FAX: 202-225-4091

Rep. Lucille Roybal-Allard (D)
(Thirty-Third District)
324 Cannon House
Office Building
Washington, D.C. 20515
Phone: 202-225-1766
FAX: 202-226-0350

Rep. Esteban E. Torres (D)
(Thirty-Fourth District)
1740 Longworth House
Office Building
Washington, D.C. 20515
Phone: 202-225-5256
FAX: 202-225-9711

Rep. Maxine Waters (D)
(Thirty-Fifth District)
1207 Longworth House
Office Building
Washington, D.C. 20515
Phone: 202-225-2201
FAX: 202-225-7854

Rep. Jane Harman (D)
(Thirty-Sixth District)
325 Cannon House
Office Building
Washington, D.C. 20515
Phone: 202-225-8220
FAX: 202-226-0684

Rep. Walter R. Tucker, III (D)
(Thirty-Seventh District)
419 Cannon House
Office Building
Washington, D.C. 20515
Phone: 202-225-7924
FAX: 202-225-7926

Rep. Steve Horn (R)
(Thirty-Eighth District)
1023 Longworth House
Office Building
Washington, D.C. 20515
Phone: 202-225-6676
FAX: 202-226-1012

Rep. Ed Royce (R)
(Thirty-Ninth District)
1404 Longworth House
Office Building
Washington, D.C. 20515
Phone: 202-225-4111
FAX: 202-226-0335

Rep. Jerry Lewis (R)
(Fortieth District)
2312 Rayburn House
Office Building
Washington, D.C. 20515
Phone: 202-225-5861
FAX: 202-225-6498

Rep. Jay C. Kim (R)
(Forty-First District)
502 Cannon House
Office Building.
Washington, D.C. 20515
Phone: 202-225-3201
FAX: 202-226-1485

Rep. George E. Brown, Jr. (D)
(Forty-Second District)
2300 Rayburn House
Office Building.
Washington, D.C. 20515
Phone: 202-225-6161
FAX: 202-225-8671

Rep. Ken Calvert (R)
(Forty-Third District)
1523 Longworth House
Office Building
Washington, D.C. 20515
Phone: 202-225-1986
FAX: (Unavailable at T.O.P.)

Rep. Sonny Bono (R)
(Forty-Fourth District)
2422 Longworth House
Office Building
Washington, D.C. 20515
Phone: 202-225-5330
FAX: 202-226-1040

Rep. Dana Rohrabacher (R)
(Forty-Fifth District)
1027 Longworth House
Office Building
Washington, D.C. 20515
Phone: 202-225-2415
FAX: 202-225-0145

Rep. Robert K. Dornan (R)
(Forty-Sixth District)
2402 Rayburn House
Office Building
Washington, D.C. 20515
Phone: 202-225-2965
FAX: 202-225-3694

Rep. C. Christopher Cox (R)
(Forty-Seventh District)
206 Cannon House
Office Building
Washington, D.C. 20515
Phone: 202-225-5611
FAX: 202-225-9177

Rep. Ronald C. Packard (R)
(Forty-Eighth District)
2162 Rayburn House
Office Building
Washington, D.C. 20515
Phone: 202-225-3906
FAX: 202-225-0134

Rep. Brian Bilbray (R)
(Forty-Ninth District)
315 Cannon House
Office Building
Washington, D.C. 20515
Phone: 202-225-2040
FAX: 202-225-2042

Rep. Bob Filner (D)
(Fiftieth District)
504 Cannon House
Office Building
Washington, D.C. 20515
Phone: 202-225-8045
FAX: 202-225-9073

Rep. Randy "Duke" Cunningham (R)
(Fifty-First District)
117 Cannon House
Office Building
Washington, D.C. 20515
Phone: 202-225-5452
FAX: 202-225-2558

Rep. Duncan Lee Hunter (R)
(Fifty-Second District)
133 Cannon House
Office Building
Washington, D.C. 20515
Phone: 202-225-5672
FAX: 202-225-0235

COLORADO

Senators
Senator Ben Nighthorse Campbell (R)
380 Russell Senate
Office Building
Washington, D.C. 20510
Phone: 202-224-5852
FAX: 202-224-3714

Senator Hank Brown (R)
716 Hart Senate
Office Building
Washington, D.C. 20510
Phone: 202-224-5941
FAX: 202-224-6471

Representatives
Rep. Patricia S. Schroeder (D)
(First District)
2208 Rayburn House
Office Building
Washington, D.C. 20515
Phone: 202-225-4431
FAX: 202-225-5842

Rep. David E. Skaggs (D)
(Second District)
1124 Longworth House
Office Building
Washington, D.C. 20515
Phone: 202-225-2161
FAX: 202-225-9127

Rep. Scott McInnis (R)
(Third District)
512 Cannon House
Office Building
Washington, D.C. 20515
Phone: 202-225-4761
FAX: 202-226-0622

Rep. Wayne Allard (R)
(Fourth District)
422 Cannon House
Office Building
Washington, D.C. 20515
Phone: 202-225-4676
FAX: 202-225-8630

Rep. Joel Hefley (R)
(Fifth District)
2442 Rayburn House
Office Building
Washington, D.C. 20515
Phone: 202-225-4422
FAX: 202-225-1942

Rep. Dan L. Schaefer (R)
(Sixth District)
2448 Rayburn House
Office Building
Washington, D.C. 20515
Phone: 202-225-7882
FAX: 202-225-7885

CONNECTICUT

Senators
Senator Christopher J. Dodd (D)
444 Russell Senate
Office Building
Washington, D.C. 20510
Phone: 202-224-2823
FAX: 202-224-5431

Senator Joseph I. Lieberman (D)
316 Hart Senate
Office Building
Washington, D.C. 20510
Phone: 202-224-4041
FAX: 202-224-9750

Representatives
Rep. Barbara B. Kennelly (D)
(First District)
201 Cannon House
Office Building
Washington, D.C. 20515
Phone: 202-225-2265
FAX: 202-225-1031

Rep. Samuel Gejdenson (D)
(Second District)
2416 Rayburn House
Office Building
Washington, D.C. 20515
Phone: 202-225-2076
FAX: 202-225-4977

Rep. Rosa DeLauro (D)
(Third District)
327 Cannon House
Office Building
Washington, D.C. 20515
Phone: 202-225-3661
FAX: 202-225-4890

Rep. Christopher Shays (R)
(Fourth District)
1034 Longworth House
Office Building
Washington, D.C. 20515
Phone: 202-225-5541
FAX: 202-225-9629

Rep. Gary Franks (R)
(Fifth District)
435 Cannon House
Office Building
Washington, D.C. 20515
Phone: 202-225-3822
FAX: 202-225-5085

Rep. Nancy Lee Johnson (R)
(Sixth District)
343 Cannon House
Office Building
Washington, D.C. 20515
Phone: 202-225-4476
FAX: 202-225-4488

DELAWARE

Senators
Senator William V. Roth, Jr. (R)
104 Hart Senate
Office Building
Washington, D.C. 20510
Phone: 202-224-2441
FAX: 202-224-2805

Senator Joseph R. Biden, Jr. (D)
221 Russell Senate
Office Building
Washington, D.C. 20510
Phone: 202-224-5042
FAX: 202-224-0139

Representative At Large
Rep. Michael N. Castle (R)
1205 Longworth House
Office Building
Washington, D.C. 20515
Phone: 202-225-4165
FAX: 202-225-2291

FLORIDA

Senators
Senator Robert Graham (D)
524 Hart Senate
Office Building
Washington, D.C. 20510
Phone: 202-224-3041
FAX: 202-224-2237

Senator Connie Mack, III (R)
517 Hart Senate
Office Building
Washington, D.C. 20510
Phone: 202-224-5274
FAX: 202-224-9365

Representatives
Rep. Joe Scarborough (D)
(First District)
2435 Rayburn House
Office Building
Washington, D.C. 20515
Phone: 202-225-4136
FAX: 202-225-5785

Rep. Pete Peterson (D)
(Second District)
426 Cannon House
Office Building
Washington, D.C. 20515
Phone: 202-225-5235
FAX: 202-225-1586

Rep. Corrine Brown (D)
(Third District)
1037 Longworth House
Office Building
Washington, D.C. 20515
Phone: 202-225-0123
FAX: 202-225-2256

Rep. Tillie Fowler (R)
(Fourth District)
413 Cannon House
Office Building
Washington, D.C. 20515
Phone: 202-225-2501
FAX: 202-226-9318

Rep. Karen L. Thurman (D)
(Fifth District)
130 Cannon House
Office Building
Washington, D.C. 20515
Phone: 202-225-1002
FAX: 202-226-0329

Rep. Cliff Stearns (R)
(Sixth District)
332 Cannon House
Office Building, #2015
Phone: 202-225-5744
FAX: 202-225-3973

Rep. John L. Mica (R)
(Seventh District)
427 Cannon House
Office Building
Washington, D.C. 20515
Phone: 202-225-4035
FAX: 202-226-0821

Rep. Bill McCollum (R)
(Eighth District)
2266 Rayburn House
Office Building
Washington, D.C. 20515
Phone: 202-225-2176
FAX: 202-225-0999

Rep. Michael Bilirakis (R) (Ninth District)
2240 Rayburn House
Office Building
Washington, D.C. 20515
Phone: 202-225-5755
FAX: 202-225-4085

Rep. C. W. Bill Young (R)
(Tenth District)
2407 Rayburn House
Office Building
Washington, D.C. 20515
Phone: 202-225-5961
FAX: 202-225-9764

Rep. Sam M. Gibbons (D)
(Eleventh District)
2204 Rayburn House
Office Building
Washington, D.C. 20515
Phone: 202-225-3376
FAX: (Unlisted)

Rep. Charles T. Canady (R)
(Twelfth District)
1107 Longworth House
Office Building
Washington, D.C. 20515
Phone: 202-225-1252
FAX: 202-225-2279

Rep. Dan Miller (R)
(Thirteenth District)
510 Cannon House Office Building
Washington, D.C. 20515
Phone: 202-225-5015
FAX: 202-226-0828

Rep. Porter Goss (R)
(Fourteenth District)
330 Cannon House Office Building
Washington, D.C. 20515
Phone: 202-225-2536
FAX: 202-225-6820

Rep. Dave Weldon (R)
(Fifteenth District)
432 Cannon House Office Building
Washington, D.C. 20515
Phone: 202-225-3671
FAX: 202-225-9039

Rep. Mark Foley (R)
(Sixteenth District)
2351 Rayburn House
Office Building
Washington, D.C. 20515
Phone: 202-225-5792
FAX: 202-225-1860

Rep. Carrie Meek (D)
(Seventeenth District)
404 Cannon House
Office Building
Washington, D.C. 20515
Phone: 202-225-4506
FAX: 202-226-0777

Rep. Ileana Ros-Lehtinen (R)
(Eighteenth District)
127 Cannon House
Office Building
Washington, D.C. 20515
Phone: 202-225-3931
FAX: 202-225-5620

Rep. Harry A. Johnston, II (D)
(Nineteenth District)
204 Cannon House Office Building
Washington, D.C. 20515
Phone: 202-225-3001
FAX: 202-225-8791

Rep. Peter Deustch (D)
(Twentieth District)
425 Cannon House Office Building
Washington, D.C. 20515
Phone: 202-225-7931
FAX: 202-225-8456

Rep. Lincoln Diaz-Balart (R)
(Twenty-First District)
509 Cannon House Office Building
Washington, D.C. 20515
Phone: 202-225-4211
FAX: 202-225-8576

Rep. E. Clay Shaw, Jr. (R)
(Twenty-Second District)
2267 Rayburn House
Office Building
Washington, D.C. 20515
Phone: 202-225-3026
FAX: 202-225-8398

Rep. Alcee L. Hastings (D)
(Twenty-Third District)
1039 Longworth House
Office Building
Washington, D.C. 20515
Phone: 202-225-1313
FAX: 202-226-0690

GEORGIA

Senators
Senator Samuel A. Nunn (D)
303 Dirksen Senate Office Building
Washington, D.C. 20510
Phone: 202-224-3521
FAX: 202-224-0072

Senator Paul Coverdell (R)
200 Russell Senate Office Building
Washington, D.C. 20510
Phone: 202-224-3643
FAX: 202-224-8227

Representatives
Rep. Jack Kingston (R)
(First District)
1229 Longworth House
Office Building
Washington, D.C. 20515
Phone: 202-225-5831
FAX: 202-226-2269

Rep. Sanford Bishop (D)
(Second District)
1632 Longworth House
Office Building
Washington, D.C. 20515
Phone: 202-225-3631
FAX: 202-225-2203

Rep. Mac Collins (R)
(Third District)
1118 Longworth House
Office Building
Washington, D.C. 20515
Phone: 202-225-5901
FAX: 202-225-2515

Rep. John Linder (R)
(Fourth District)
1605 Longworth House
Office Building
Washington, D.C. 20515
Phone: 202-225-4272
FAX: 202-225-4696

Rep. John R. Lewis (D)
(Fifth District)
329 Cannon House
Office Building
Washington, D.C. 20515
Phone: 202-225-3801
FAX: 202-225-0351

Rep. Newton L. Gingrich (R)
(Sixth District)
2428 Rayburn House
Office Building
Washington, D.C. 20515
Phone: 202-225-4501
FAX: 202-225-4656

Rep. Robert Barr (D)
(Seventh District)
2303 Rayburn House
Office Building
Washington, D.C. 20515
Phone: 202-225-2931
FAX: 202-225-0473

Rep. Saxby Chambuss (R)
(Eighth District)
2134 Rayburn House
Office Building
Washington, D.C. 20515
Phone: 202-225-6531
FAX: 202-225-7719

Rep. Nathan Deal (R)
(Ninth District)
1406 Longworth House
Office Building
Washington, D.C. 20515
Phone: 202-225-5211
FAX: 202-225-8272

Rep. Charles Norwood (R)
(Tenth District)
226 Cannon House
Office Building
Washington, D.C. 20515
Phone: 202-225-4101
FAX: 202-226-1466

Rep. Cynthia McKinney (D)
(Eleventh District)
124 Cannon House
Office Building
Washington, D.C. 20515
Phone: 202-225-1605
FAX: 202-226-0691

HAWAII

Senators
Senator Daniel K. Inouye (D)
722 Hart Senate
Office Building
Washington, D.C. 20510
Phone: 202-224-3934
FAX: 202-224-6747

Senator Daniel K. Akaka (D)
720 Hart Senate
Office Building
Washington, D.C. 20510
Phone: 202-224-6361
FAX 202-224-2126:

Representatives
Rep. Neil Abercrombie (D)
(First District)
1440 Longworth House
Office Building
Washington, D.C. 20515
Phone: 202-225-2726
FAX: 202-225-4580

Rep. Patsy T. Mink (D)
(Second District)
2135 Rayburn House
Office Building
Washington, D.C. 20515
Phone: 202-225-4906
FAX: 202-225-4987

IDAHO

Senators
Senator Dirk Kempthorne (R)
367 Dirksen Senate
Office Building
Washington, D.C. 20510
Phone: 202-224-6142
FAX: 202-224-5893

Senator Larry Craig (R)
313 Hart Senate
Office Building
Washington, D.C. 20510
Phone: 202-224-2752
FAX: 202-224-2573

Representatives
Rep. Helen Chenoweth (R)
(First District)
1117 Longworth House
Office Building
Washington, D.C. 20515
Phone: 202-225-55
FAX: 202-226-1213

Rep. Michael D. Crapo (R)
(Second District)
437 Cannon House Office Building
Washington, D.C. 20515
Phone: 202-225-5531
FAX: 202-334-1953

ILLINOIS

Senators
Senator Carol Moseley-Braun (D)
320 Hart Senate Office Building
Washington, D.C. 20510
Phone: 202-224-2854
FAX: unlisted

Senator Paul Simon (D)
462 Dirksen Senate
Office Building
Washington, D.C. 20510
Phone: 202-224-2152
FAX: 202-224-0868

Representatives
Rep. Bobby L. Rush (D)
(First District)
1725 Longworth House
Office Building
Washington, D.C. 20515
Phone: 202-225-4372
FAX: 202-226-0333

Rep. Melvin J. Reynolds (D)
(Second District)
514 Cannon House Office Building
Washington, D.C. 20515
Phone: 202-225-0773
FAX: 202-225-0774

Rep. William O. Lipinski (D)
(Third District)
1501 Longworth House
Office Building
Washington, D.C. 20515
Phone: 202-225-5701
FAX: 202-225-1012

Rep. Luis V. Gutierrez (D)
(Fourth District)
1208 Longworth House
Office Building
Washington, D.C. 20515
Phone: 202-225-8203
FAX: 202-225-7810

Rep. Michael Flanaghan (D)
(Fifth District)
2111 Rayburn House
Office Building
Washington, D.C. 20515
Phone: 202-225-4061
FAX: 202-225-4064

Rep. Henry John Hyde (R)
(Sixth District)
2110 Rayburn House
Office Building
Washington, D.C. 20515
Phone: 202-225-4561
FAX: 202-226-1240

Rep. Cardiss Collins (D)
(Seventh District)
2308 Rayburn House
Office Building
Washington, D.C. 20515
Phone: 202-225-5006
FAX: 202-225-8396

Rep. Philip Miller Crane (R)
(Eighth District)
233 Cannon House
Office Building
Washington, D.C. 20515
Phone: 202-225-3711
FAX: 202-225-7830

Rep. Sidney R. Yates (D)
(Ninth District)
2109 Rayburn House
Office Building
Washington, D.C. 20515
Phone: 202-225-2111
FAX: 202-225-3493

Rep. John E. Porter (R)
(Tenth District)
1026 Longworth House
Office Building, #2015
Phone: 202-225-4835
FAX: 202-225-0157

Rep. Gerald Weller (R)
(Eleventh District)
1032 Longworth House
Office Building
Washington, D.C. 20515
Phone: 202-225-3635
FAX: 202-225-4447

Rep. Jerry F. Costello (D)
(Twelfth District)
119 Cannon House Office Building
Washington, D.C. 20515
Phone: 202-225-5661
FAX: 202-225-0285

Rep. Harris W. Fawell (R)
(Thirteenth District)
2342 Rayburn House
Office Building
Washington, D.C. 20515
Phone: 202-225-3515
FAX: 202-225-9420

Rep. John D. Hastert (R)
(Fourteenth District)
2453 Rayburn House
Office Building
Washington, D.C. 20515
Phone: 202-225-2976
FAX: 202-225-0697

Rep. Thomas Ewing (R)
(Fifteenth District)
1317 Longworth House
Office Building
Washington, D.C. 20515
Phone: 202-225-2371
FAX: 202-225-8071

Rep. Donald Manzullo (R)
(Sixteenth District)
506 Cannon House Office Building
Washington, D.C. 20515
Phone: 202-225-5676
FAX: 202-225-5284

Rep. Lane Evans (D)
(Seventeenth District)
2335 Rayburn House
Office Building
Washington, D.C. 20515
Phone: 202-225-5905
FAX: 202-225-5396

Rep. Ray LaHood (R)
(Eighteenth District)
2112 Rayburn House
Office Building
Washington, D.C. 20515
Phone: 202-225-6201
FAX: 202-225-9249

Rep. Glenn Poshard (D)
(Nineteenth District)
107 Cannon House
Office Building
Washington, D.C. 20515
Phone: 202-225-5201
FAX: 202-225-1541

Rep. Richard J. Durbin (D)
(Twentieth District)
2463 Rayburn House
Office Building
Washington, D.C. 20515
Phone: 202-225-5271
FAX: 202-225-0170

INDIANA

Senators
Senator Richard Green Lugar (R)
306 Hart Senate Office Building
Washington, D.C. 20510
Phone: 202-224-4814
FAX: 202-224-7877

Senator Daniel R. Coats (R)
404 Russell Senate
Office Building
Washington, D.C. 20510
Phone: 202-224-5623
FAX: 202-224-1966

Representatives
Rep. Peter J. Visclosky (D)
(First District)
2464 Rayburn House
Office Building
Washington, D.C. 20515
Phone: 202-225-2461
FAX: 202-225-2493

Rep. David McIntosh (R)
(Second District)
2217 Rayburn House
Office Building
Washington, D.C. 20515
Phone: 202-225-3021
FAX: 202-225-8140

Rep. Tim Roemer (D)
(Third District)
415 Cannon House Office Building
Washington, D.C. 20515
Phone: 202-225-3915
FAX: 202-225-6798

Rep. Mark Souder (R)
(Fourth District)
1513 Longworth House
Office Building
Washington, D.C. 20515
Phone: 202-225-4436
FAX: 202-225-8810

Rep. Steve Buyer (R)
(Fifth District)
1419 Longworth House
Office Building
Washington, D.C. 20515
Phone: 202-225-5037
FAX: (Unlisted)

Rep. Dan Burton (R)
(Sixth District)
2411 Rayburn House
Office Building
Washington, D.C. 20515
Phone: 202-225-2276
FAX: 202-225-0016

Rep. John T. Myers (R)
(Seventh District)
2372 Rayburn House
Office Building
Washington, D.C. 20515
Phone: 202-225-5805
FAX: 202-225-1649

Rep. John Hostettler (R)
(Eighth District)
306 Cannon House Office Building
Washington, D.C. 20515
Phone: 202-225-4636
FAX: 202-225-4688

Rep. Lee H. Hamilton (D) (Ninth District)
2187 Rayburn House Office Building
Washington, D.C. 20515
Phone: 202-225-5315
FAX: 202-225-1101

Rep. Andrew Jacobs, Jr. (D)
(Tenth District)
2313 Rayburn House
Office Building
Washington, D.C. 20515
Phone: 202-225-4011
FAX: 202-226-4093

IOWA

Senators
Senator Charles E. Grassley (R)
135 Hart Senate Office Building
Washington, D.C. 20510
Phone: 202-224-3744
FAX: 202-224-6020

Senator Thomas R. Harkin (D)
531 Hart Senate Office Building
Washington, D.C. 20510
Phone: 202-224-3254
FAX: 202-224-9369

Representatives
Rep. James A. S. Leach (R)
(First District)
2186 Longworth House
Office Building
Washington, D.C. 20515
Phone: 202-225-6576
FAX: 202-226-1278

Rep. Jim Nussle (R)
(Second District)
308 Cannon House
Office Building
Washington, D.C. 20515
Phone: 202-225-2911
FAX: 202-225-9129

Rep. James R. Lightfoot (R)
(Third District)
2444 Rayburn House
Office Building
Washington, D.C. 20515
Phone: 202-225-3806
FAX: 202-225-6973

Rep. Greg Ganske (R)
(Fourth District)
2373 Rayburn House
Office Building
Washington, D.C. 20515
Phone: 202-225-4426
FAX: (Unlisted)

Rep. Tom Latham (R)
(Fifth District)
418 Cannon House
Office Building
Washington, D.C. 20515
Phone: 202-225-5476
FAX: 202-225-5796

KANSAS

Senators
Senator Robert Dole (R)
141 Hart Senate Office Building
Washington, D.C. 20510
Phone: 202-224-6521
FAX: 202-224-8952

Senator Nancy Landon Kassebaum (R)
302 Russell Senate
Office Building
Washington, D.C. 20510
Phone: 202-224-4774
FAX: 202-224-3514

Representatives
Rep. Charles P. Roberts (R)
(First District)
1125 Longworth House
Office Building
Washington, D.C. 20515
Phone: 202-225-2715
FAX: 202-225-5375

Rep. Sam Brownback (R)
(Second District)
2243 Longworth House
Office Building
Washington, D.C. 20515
Phone: 202-225-6601
FAX: 202-225-1445

Rep. Jan Meyers (R)
(Third District)
2338 Rayburn House
Office Building
Washington, D.C. 20515
Phone: 202-225-2865
FAX: 202-225-0554

Rep. Todd Tiahrt (R)
(Fourth District)
2371 Rayburn House
Office Building
Washington, D.C. 20515
Phone: 202-225-6216
FAX: 202-225-5398

KENTUCKY

Senators
Senator Wendell Hampton Ford (D)
173A Russell Senate
Office Building
Washington, D.C. 20510
Phone: 202-224-4343
FAX: 202-224-1144

Senator Mitch McConnell (R)
120 Russell Senate Office Building
Washington, D.C. 20510
Phone: 202-224-2541
FAX: 202-224-2499

Representatives
Rep. Edward Whitfield (R)
(First District)
1533 Longworth House
Office Building
Washington, D.C. 20515
Phone: 202-225-3115
FAX: 202-225-2169

Rep. Ron Lewis (R)
(Second District)
2333 Rayburn House
Office Building
Washington, D.C. 20515
Phone: 202-225-3501
FAX: (Unlisted)

Rep. Mike Ward (D)
(Third District)
2246 Rayburn House
Office Building
Washington, D.C. 20515
Phone: 202-225-5401
FAX:

Rep. Jim Bunning (R)
(Fourth District)
2437 Rayburn House
Office Building
Washington, D.C. 20515
Phone: 202-225-3465
FAX: 202-225-0003

Rep. Harold D. Rogers (R)
(Fifth District)
2468 Cannon House
Office Building
Washington, D.C. 20515
Phone: 202-225-4601
FAX: 202-225-0940

Rep. Scotty Baesler (D)
(Sixth District)
508 Cannon House
Office Building
Washington, D.C. 20515
Phone: 202-225-4706
FAX: 202-225-2122

LOUISIANA

Senators
Senator J. Bennett Johnston, Jr. (D)
136 Hart Senate
Office Building
Washington, D.C. 20510
Phone: 202-224-5824
FAX: 202-224-2952

Senator John B. Breaux (D)
516 Hart Senate Office Building
Washington, D.C. 20510
Phone: 202-224-4623
FAX: 202-224-2435

Representatives
Rep. Robert Livingston, Jr. (R)
(First District)
2368 Longworth House
Office Building
Washington, D.C. 20515
Phone: 202-225-3015
FAX: 202-225-0739

Rep. William J. Jefferson (D)
(Second District)
428 Cannon House
Office Building
Washington, D.C. 20515
Phone: 202-225-6636
FAX: 202-225-1988

Rep. W. J. "Billy" Tauzin (R)
(Third District)
2330 Rayburn House
Office Building
Washington, D.C. 20515
Phone: 202-225-4031
FAX: 202-225-0563

Rep. Cleo Fields (D)
(Fourth District)
513 Cannon House
Office Building
Washington, D.C. 20515
Phone: 202-225-8490
FAX: 220-225-8959

Rep. James O. McCrery, III (R)
(Fifth District)
225 Cannon House Office Building
Washington, D.C. 20515
Phone: 202-225-2777
FAX: 202-225-8039

Rep. Richard H. Baker (R)
(Sixth District)
434 Cannon House
Office Building
Washington, D.C. 20515
Phone: 202-225-3901
FAX: 202-225-7313

Rep. James A. Hayes (D)
(Seventh District)
2432 Rayburn House
Office Building
Washington, D.C. 20515
Phone: 202-225-2031
FAX: 202-225-1175

MAINE

Senators
Senator William S. Cohen (R)
322 Hart Senate Office Building
Washington, D.C. 20510
Phone: 202-224-2523
FAX: 202-224-2693

Senator Olympia Snowe (R)
176 Russell Senate
Office Building
Washington, D.C. 20510
Phone: 202-224-5344
FAX: 202-224-6853

Representatives
Rep. James Longley (R)
(First District)
1530 Longworth House
Office Building
Washington, D.C. 20515
Phone: 202-225-6116
FAX: 202-225-9065

Rep. John Baldacci (D)
(Second District)
2268 Rayburn House
Office Building
Washington, D.C. 20515
Phone: 202-225-6306
FAX: 202-225-8297

MARYLAND

Senators
Senator Paul S. Sarbanes (D)
309 Hart Senate Office Building
Washington, D.C. 20510
Phone: 202-224-4524
FAX: 202-224-1651

Senator Barbara A. Mikulski (D)
709 Hart Senate Office Building
Washington, D.C. 20510
Phone: 202-224-4654
FAX: 202-224-8858

Representatives
Rep. Wayne T. Gilchrest (R) (First District)
412 Cannon House Office Building
Washington, D.C. 20515
Phone: 202-225-5311
FAX: 202-225-0254

Rep. Robert Erlich (R)
(Second District)
1610 Longworth House
Office Building
Washington, D.C. 20515
Phone: 202-225-3061
FAX: 202-225-4251

Rep. Benjamin L. Cardin (D)
(Third District)
227 Cannon House
Office Building
Washington, D.C. 20515
Phone: 202-225-4016
FAX: 202-225-9219

Rep. Albert R. Wynn (D)
(Fourth District)
423 Cannon House
Office Building
Washington, D.C. 20515
Phone: 202-225-8699
FAX: 202-225-8714

Rep. Steny H. Hoyer (D)
(Fifth District)
1705 Longworth House
Office Building
Washington, D.C. 20515
Phone: 202-225-4131
FAX: 202-225-4300

Rep. Roscoe Bartlett (R)
(Sixth District)
312 Cannon House Office Building
Washington, D.C. 20515
Phone: 202-225-2721
FAX: 202-225-2193

Rep. Kweisi Mfume (D)
(Seventh District)
2419 Rayburn House
Office Building
Washington, D.C. 20515
Phone: 202-225-4741
FAX: 202-225-3178

Rep. Constance A. Morella (R)
(Eighth District)
223 Cannon House
Office Building
Washington, D.C. 20515
Phone: 202-225-5341
FAX: 202-225-1389

MASSACHUSETTS

Senators
Senator Edward M. Kennedy (D)
315 Russell Senate
Office Building
Washington, D.C. 20510
Phone: 202-224-4543
FAX: 202-224-2417

Senator John Kerry (D)
421 Russell Senate
Office Building
Washington, D.C. 20510
Phone: 202-224-2742
FAX: 202-224-8525

Representatives
Rep. John W. Olver (D)
(First District)
1323 Longworth House
Office Building
Washington, D.C. 20515
Phone: 202-225-5335
FAX: 202-226-1224

Rep. Richard E. Neal (D)
(Second District)
131 Cannon House
Office Building
Washington, D.C. 20515
Phone: 202-225-5601
FAX: 202-225-8112

Rep. Peter I. Blute (R)
(Third District)
1029 Longworth House
Office Building
Washington, D.C. 20515
Phone: 202-225-6101
FAX: 202-225-2217

Rep. Barney Frank (D)
(Fourth District)
2404 Rayburn House
Office Building
Washington, D.C. 20515
Phone: 202-225-5931
FAX: 202-225-0182

Rep. Martin T. Meehan (D)
(Fifth District)
1223 Longworth House
Office Building
Washington, D.C. 20515
Phone: 202-225-3411
FAX: 202-225-0771

Rep. Peter G. Torkildsen (R)
(Sixth District)
120 Cannon House
Office Building
Washington, D.C. 20515
Phone: 202-225-8020
FAX: 202-225-8037

Rep. Edward J. Markey (D)
(Seventh District)
2133 Rayburn House
Office Building
Washington, D.C. 20515
Phone: 202-225-2836
FAX: 202-225-8689

Rep. Joseph P. Kennedy, II (D)
(Eighth District)
1210 Longworth House
Office Building
Washington, D.C. 20515
Phone: 202-225-5111
FAX: 202-225-9322

Rep. John J. Moakley (D)
(Ninth District)
235 Cannon House
Office Building
Washington, D.C. 20515
Phone: 202-225-8273
FAX: 202-225-3984

Rep. Gerry E. Studds (D)
(Tenth District)
237 Cannon House
Office Building
Washington, D.C. 20515
Phone: 202-225-3111
FAX: 202-225-2212

MICHIGAN

Senators
Senator Spencer Abraham (R)
105 Dirksen Senate
Office Building
Washington, D.C. 20510
Phone: 202-224-4822
FAX: 202-224-8834

Senator Carl M. Levin (D)
459 Russell Senate
Office Building
Washington, D.C. 20510
Phone: 202-224-6221
FAX: 202-224-5908

Representatives
Rep. Bart Stupak (D)
(First District)
317 Cannon House
Office Building
Washington, D.C. 20515
Phone: 202-225-4735
FAX: 202-225-4744

Rep. Peter Hoekstra (R)
(Second District)
1319 Longworth House
Office Building
Washington, D.C. 20515
Phone: 202-225-4401
FAX: 202-226-0779

Rep. Vernon Ehlers (R)
(Third District)
1526 Longworth House
Office Building
Washington, D.C. 20515
Phone: 202-225-3831
FAX: (Unlisted)

Rep. David Camp (R)
(Fourth District)
137 Cannon House
Office Building
Washington, D.C. 20515
Phone: 202-225-3561
FAX: 202-225-9679

Rep. James A. Barcia (D)
(Fifth District)
1717 Longworth House
Office Building
Washington, D.C. 20515
Phone: 202-225-8171
FAX: 202-225-2168

Rep. Frederick S. Upton (R)
(Sixth District)
2439 Longworth House
Office Building
Washington, D.C. 20515
Phone: 202-225-3761
FAX: 202-225-4986

Rep. Nick Smith (R)
(Seventh District)
1708 Longworth House
Office Building
Washington, D.C. 20515
Phone: 202-225-6276
FAX: 202-225-6281

Rep. Dick Chrysler (R)
(Eighth District)
2347 Rayburn House
Office Building
Washington, D.C. 20515
Phone: 202-225-4872
FAX: 202-225-1260

Rep. Dale E. Kildee (D)
(Ninth District)
2239 Rayburn House
Office Building
Washington, D.C. 20515
Phone: 202-225-3611
FAX: 202-225-6393

Rep. David E. Bonior (D)
(Tenth District)
2207 Rayburn House
Office Building
Washington, D.C. 20515
Phone: 202-225-2106
FAX: 202-226-1169

Rep. Joe Knollenberg (R)
(Eleventh District)
1218 Longworth House
Office Building
Washington, D.C. 20515
Phone: 202-225-5802
FAX: 202-226-2356

Rep. Sander Martin Levin (D)
(Twelfth District)
106 Cannon House
Office Building
Washington, D.C. 20515
Phone: 202-225-4961
FAX: 202-226-1033

Rep. Lynn Rivers (D)
(Thirteenth District)
2107 Rayburn House
Office Building
Washington, D.C. 20515
Phone: 202-225-6261
FAX: 202-225-0489

Rep. John Conyers, Jr. (D)
(Fourteenth District)
Rayburn House
Office Building
Washington, D.C. 20515
Phone: 202-225-5126
FAX: 202-225-0072

Rep. Barbara-Rose Collins (D)
(Fifteenth District)
1108 Longworth House
Office Building
Washington, D.C. 20515
Phone: 202-225-2261
FAX: 202-225-6645

Rep. John D. Dingell (D) (Sixteenth District)
2328 Rayburn House
Office Building
Washington, D.C. 20515
Phone: 202-225-4071
FAX: 202-225-7426

MINNESOTA

Senators
Senator Rod Grams (R)
154 Russell Senate
Office Building
Washington, D.C. 20510
Phone: 202-224-3244
FAX: 202-224-9931

Senator Paul Wellstone (DFL)
717 Hart Senate
Office Building
Washington, D.C. 20510
Phone: 202-224-5641
FAX: 202-224-8438

Representatives
Rep. Gil Gutknecht (DFL)
(First District)
436 Cannon House
Office Building
Washington, D.C. 20515
Phone: 202-225-2472
FAX: 202-225-0051

Rep. David Minge (D)
(Second District)
1508 Longworth House
Office Building
Washington, D.C. 20515
Phone: 202-225-2331
FAX: 202-226-0836

Rep. James Ramstad (R)
(Third District)
322 Cannon House
Office Building
Washington, D.C. 20515
Phone: 202-225-2871
FAX: 202-225-6351

Rep. Bruce F. Vento (DFL)
(Fourth District)
2304 Rayburn House
Office Building
Washington, D.C. 20515
Phone: 202-225-6631
FAX: 202-225-1968

Rep. Martin Olav Sabo (DFL)
(Fifth District)
2336 Rayburn House
Office Building
Washington, D.C. 20515
Phone: 202-225-4755
FAX: 202-225-4886

Rep. William Luther (D)
(Sixth District)
1713 Longworth House
Office Building
Washington, D.C. 20515
Phone: 202-225-2271
FAX: 202-225-9802

Rep. Collin C. Peterson (DFL)
(Seventh District)
1133 Longworth House
Office Building
Washington, D.C. 20515
Phone: 202-225-2165
FAX: 202-225-1593

Rep. James L. Oberstar (DFL)
(Eighth District)
2366 Rayburn House
Office Building
Washington, D.C. 20515
Phone: 202-225-6211
FAX: 202-225-0699

MISSISSIPPI

Senators
Senator Thad Cochran (R)
326 Russell Senate
Office Building
Washington, D.C. 20510
Phone: 202-224-5054
FAX: 202-224-3576

Senator Trent Lott (R)
487 Russell Senate
Office Building
Washington, D.C. 20510
Phone: 202-224-6253
FAX: 202-224-2262

Representatives
Rep. Roger Wicker (R)
(First District)
2314 Rayburn House
Office Building
Washington, D.C. 20515
Phone: 202-225-4306
FAX: 202-225-4328

Rep. Bernie Thompson (D)
(Second District)
1408 Longworth House
Office Building
Washington, D.C. 20515
Phone: 202-225-5876
FAX: 202-225-5898

**Rep. G. V. "Sonny" Montgomery
(D)** (Third District)
2184 Rayburn House
Office Building
Washington, D.C. 20515
Phone: 202-225-5031
FAX: 202-225-3375

Rep. Mike Parker (D)
(Fourth District)
1410 Longworth House
Office Building
Washington, D.C. 20515
Phone: 202-225-5865
FAX: 202-225-5886

Rep. Gene Taylor (D)
(Fifth District)
214 Cannon House
Office Building
Washington, D.C. 20515
Phone: 202-225-5772
FAX: 202-225-7074

MISSOURI

Senators
Senator John Ashcroft (R)
249 Russell Senate
Office Building
Washington, D.C. 20510
Phone: 202-224-6154
FAX: 202-224-7615

Senator Christopher Samuel "Kit" Bond (R)
293 Russell Senate
Office Building
Washington, D.C. 20510
Phone: 202-224-5721
FAX: 202-224-7491

Representatives
Rep. William L. Clay (D)
(First District)
2306 Rayburn House
Office Building
Washington, D.C. 20515
Phone: 202-225-2406
FAX: 202-225-1725

Rep. James M. Talent (R)
(Second District)
1022 Longworth House
Office Building
Washington, D.C. 20515
Phone: 202-225-2561
FAX: 202-225-2563

Rep. Richard A. Gephardt (D)
(Third District)
1432 Longworth House
Office Building
Washington, D.C. 20515
Phone: 202-225-2671
FAX: 202-225-7414

Rep. Isaac "Ike" Skelton, IV (D)
(Fourth District)
2227 Rayburn House
Office Building
Washington, D.C. 20515
Phone: 202-225-2876
FAX: 202-225-2695

Rep. Karen McCarthy (D)
(Fifth District)
2334 Rayburn House
Office Building
Washington, D.C. 20515
Phone: 202-225-4535
FAX: 202-225-5990

Rep. Pat Danner (D)
(Sixth District)
1217 Longworth House
Office Building
Washington, D.C. 20515
Phone: 202-225-7041
FAX: 202-225-8221

Rep. Melton D. Hancock (R)
(Seventh District)
129 Cannon House
Office Building
Washington, D.C. 20515
Phone: 202-225-6536
FAX: 202-225-7700

Rep. Bill Emerson (R)
(Eighth District)
2454 Cannon House
Office Building
Washington, D.C. 20515
Phone: 202-225-4404
FAX: 202-225-9621

Rep. Harold L. Volkmer (D)
(Ninth District)
2409 Rayburn House
Office Building
Washington, D.C. 20515
Phone: 202-225-2956
FAX: 202-225-7834

MONTANA

Senators
Senator Max Baucus (D)
511 Hart Senate
Office Building
Washington, D.C. 20510
Phone: 202-224-2651
FAX: (Unavailable at T.O.P.)

Senator Conrad Burns (R)
183 Dirksen Senate
Office Building
Washington, D.C. 20510
Phone: 202-224-2644
FAX: 202-224-8594

Representative At Large
Rep. Pat Williams (D)
2457 Rayburn House
Office Building
Washington, D.C. 20515
Phone: 202-225-3211
FAX: 202-226-0244

NEBRASKA

Senators
Senator J. James Exon (D)
528 Hart Senate
Office Building
Washington, D.C. 20510
Phone: 202-224-4224
FAX: 202-224-5213

Senator Joseph R. Kerrey (D)
303 Hart Senate
Office Building
Washington, D.C. 20510
Phone: 202-224-6551
FAX: 202-224-7645

Representatives
Rep. Douglas K. Bereuter (R)
(First District)
2348 Rayburn House
Office Building
Washington, D.C. 20515
Phone: 202-225-4806
FAX: 202-226-1148

Rep. Jon Christensen (R)
(Second District)
1113 Longworth House
Office Building
Washington, D.C. 20515
Phone: 202-225-4155
FAX: 202-225-4684

Rep. William Barrett (R)
(Third District)
1213 Longworth House
Office Building
Washington, D.C. 20515
Phone: 202-225-6435
FAX: 202-225-0207

NEVADA

Senators
Senator Harry M. Reid (D)
324 Hart Senate
Office Building
Washington, D.C. 20510
Phone: 202-224-3542
FAX: 202-224-7327

Senator Richard H. Bryan (D)
364 Russell Senate
Office Building
Washington, D.C. 20510
Phone: 202-224-6244
FAX: 202-224-1867

Representatives
Rep. John Ensign (D)
(First District)
2431 Rayburn House
Office Building
Washington, D.C. 20515
Phone: 202-255-5965
FAX: 202-225-8808

Rep. Barbara F. Vucanovich (R)
(Second District)
2202 Rayburn House Office Building
Washington, D.C. 20515
Phone: 202-225-6155
FAX: 202-225-2319

NEW HAMPSHIRE

Senators
Senator Judd Gregg (R)
393 Russell Senate
Office Building
Washington, D.C. 20510
Phone: 202-224-3324
FAX: 202-224-4952

Senator Robert C. Smith (R)
332 Dirksen Senate
Office Building
Washington, D.C. 20510
Phone: 202-224-2841
FAX: 202-224-1353

Representatives
Rep. William Zeliff (R)
(First District)
224 Cannon House
Office Building
Washington, D.C. 20515
Phone: 202-225-5456
FAX: 202-225-4370

Rep. Charles Bass (R)
(Second District)
230 Cannon House
Office Building
Washington, D.C. 20515
Phone: 202-225-5206
FAX: 202-225-0046

NEW JERSEY

Senators
Senator Bill Bradley (D)
731 Hart Senate
Office Building
Washington, D.C. 20510
Phone: 202-224-3224
FAX: 202-224-8567

Senator Frank R. Lautenberg (D)
506 Hart Senate
Office Building
Washington, D.C. 20510
Phone: 202-224-4744
FAX: 202-224-9707

Representatives
Rep. Robert E. Andrews (D)
(First District)
1005 Longworth House
Office Building
Washington, D.C. 20515
Phone: 202-225-6501
FAX: 202-225-6583

Rep. Frank LoBiondo (R)
(Second District)
241 Cannon House
Office Building
Washington, D.C. 20515
Phone: 202-225-6572
FAX: 202-225-8530

Rep. H. James Saxton (R)
(Third District)
438 Cannon House
Office Building
Washington, D.C. 20515
Phone: 202-225-4765
FAX: 202-225-0778

Rep. Christopher H. Smith (R)
(Fourth District)
2353 Rayburn House
Office Building
Washington, D.C. 20515
Phone: 202-225-3765
FAX: 202-225-7768

Rep. Marge S. Roukema (R)
(Fifth District)
2244 Rayburn House
Office Building
Washington, D.C. 20515
Phone: 202-225-4465
FAX: 202-225-9048

Rep. Frank J. Pallone, Jr. (D)
(Sixth District)
420 Cannon House
Office Building
Washington, D.C. 20515
Phone: 202-225-4671
FAX: 202-225-9665

Rep. Bob Franks (R)
(Seventh District)
429 Cannon House
Office Building
Washington, D.C. 20515
Phone: 202-225-5361
FAX: 202-225-9460

Rep. Bill Martini (R)
(Eighth District)
1728 Longworth House
Office Building
Washington, D.C. 20515
Phone: 202-225-5751
FAX: 202-226-2273

Rep. Robert G. Torricelli (D)
(Ninth District)
2159 Rayburn House
Office Building
Washington, D.C. 20515
Phone: 202-225-5061
FAX: 202-225-0843

Rep. Donald M. Payne (D)
(Tenth District)
417 Cannon House
Office Building
Washington, D.C. 20515
Phone: 202-225-3436
FAX: 202-225-4160

Rep. Rodney Frelinghuysen (R)
(Eleventh District)
2447 Rayburn House
Office Building
Washington, D.C. 20515
Phone: 202-225-5034
FAX: 202-225-0658

Rep. Richard Zimmer (R)
(Twelfth District)
228 Cannon House
Office Building
Washington, D.C. 20515
Phone: 202-225-5801
FAX: 202-226-0792

Rep. Robert Menendez (D)
(Thirteenth District)
1531 Longworth House
Office Building
Washington, D.C. 20515
Phone: 202-225-7919
FAX: 202-22-0792

NEW MEXICO

Senators
Senator Pete V. Domenici (R)
427 Dirksen Senate
Office Building
Washington, D.C. 20510
Phone: 202-224-6621
FAX: 202-224-7371

Senator Jeff Bingaman (D)
524 Hart Senate Office Building
Washington, D.C. 20510
Phone: 202-224-5521
FAX: 202-224-1810

Representatives
Rep. Steven H. Schiff (R)
(First District)
1009 Longworth House
Office Building
Washington, D.C. 20515
Phone: 202-225-6316
FAX: 202-225-4975

Rep. Joseph R. Skeen (R)
(Second District)
2367 Rayburn House
Office Building
Washington, D.C. 20515
Phone: 202-225-2365
FAX: 202-225-9599

Rep. Bill Richardson (D)
(Third District)
2349 Rayburn House
Office Building
Washington, D.C. 20515
Phone: 202-225-6190
FAX: 202-225-1950

NEW YORK

Senators
Senator Daniel Patrick Moynihan (D)
464 Russell Senate
Office Building
Washington, D.C. 20510
Phone: 202-224-4451
FAX: 202-224-9293

Senator Alfonse M. D'Amato (R)
520 Hart Senate
Office Building
Washington, D.C. 20510
Phone: 202-224-6542
FAX: 202-224-5871

Representatives
Rep. Michael Forbes (R)
(First District)
229 Cannon House
Office Building
Washington, D.C. 20515
Phone: 202-225-3826
FAX: 202-225-0776

Rep. Rick Lazio (R)
(Second District)
314 Cannon House
Office Building
Washington, D.C. 20515
Phone: 202-225-3335
FAX: 202-225-4669

Rep. Peter King (R)
(Third District)
118 Cannon House
Office Building
Washington, D.C. 20515
Phone: 202-225-7896
FAX: 202-226-2279

Rep. Daniel Frisa (R)
(Fourth District)
116 Cannon House
Office Building
Washington, D.C. 20515
Phone: 202-225-5516
FAX: 202-225-4672

Rep. Gary L. Ackerman (D)
(Fifth District)
2445 Rayburn House
Office Building
Washington, D.C. 20515
Phone: 202-225-2601
FAX: 202-225-1589

Rep. Floyd H. Flake (D)
(Sixth District)
1035 Longworth House
Office Building
Washington, D.C. 20515
Phone: 202-225-3461
FAX: 202-225-4169

Rep. Thomas J. Manton (D)
(Seventh District)
203 Cannon House
Office Building
Washington, D.C. 20515
Phone: 202-225-3965
FAX: 202-225-1909

Rep. Jerrold Nadler (D)
(Eighth District)
424 Cannon House
Office Building
Washington, D.C. 20515
Phone: 202-225-5635
FAX: 202-225-6923

Rep. Charles E. Schumer (D)
(Ninth District)
2412 Longworth House
Office Building
Washington, D.C. 20515
Phone: 202-225-6616
FAX: 202-225-4183

Rep. Edolphus Towns (D)
(Tenth District)
2232 Rayburn House
Office Building
Washington, D.C. 20515
Phone: 202-225-5936
FAX: 202-225-1018

Rep. Major R. Owens (D)
(Eleventh District)
2305 Rayburn House
Office Building.
Washington, D.C. 20515
Phone: 202-225-6231
FAX: 202-226-0112

Rep. Nydia Velazquez (D)
(Twelfth District)
132 Cannon House
Office Building
Washington, D.C. 20515
Phone: 202-225-2361
FAX: 202-226-0327

Rep. Susan Molinari (R)
(Thirteenth District)
123 Cannon House
Office Building
Washington, D.C. 20515
Phone: 202-225-3371
FAX: 202-226-1272

Rep. Carolyn Maloney (D)
(Fourteenth District)
1504 Longworth House
Office Building
Washington, D.C. 20515
Phone: 202-225-7944
FAX: 202-225-4709

Rep. Charles Bernard Rangel (D)
(Fifteenth District)
2252 Rayburn House
Office Building
Washington, D.C. 20515
Phone: 202-225-4365
FAX: 202-225-0816

Rep. Jose E. Serrano (D)
(Sixteenth District)
336 Cannon House
Office Building
Washington, D.C. 20515
Phone: 202-225-4361
FAX: 202-225-6001

Rep. Eliot L. Engel (D)
(Seventeenth District)
1434 Longworth House
Office Building
Washington, D.C. 20515
Phone: 202-225-2464
FAX: 202-225-5513

Rep. Nita M. Lowey (D)
(Eighteenth District)
1424 Longworth House
Office Building
Washington, D.C. 20515
Phone: 202-225-6506
FAX: 202-225-0546

Rep. Sue Kelly (R)
(Nineteenth District)
2354 Rayburn House
Office Building
Washington, D.C. 20515
Phone: 202-225-5441
FAX: 202-225-0962

Rep. Benjamin A. Gilman (R)
(Twentieth District)
2185 Rayburn House
Office Building
Washington, D.C. 20515
Phone: 202-225-3776
FAX: 202-225-2541

Rep. Michael R. McNulty (D)
(Twenty-First District)
217 Cannon House
Office Building
Washington, D.C. 20515
Phone: 202-225-5076
FAX: 202-225-5077

Rep. Gerald B. H. Solomon (R)
(Twenty-Second District)
2265 Rayburn House
Office Building
Washington, D.C. 20515
Phone: 202-225-5614
FAX: 202-225-5234

Rep. Sherwood L. Boehlert (R)
(Twenty-Third District)
1127 Longworth House
Office Building
Washington, D.C. 20515
Phone: 202-225-3665
FAX: 202-225-1891

Rep. John McHugh (R)
(Twenty-Fourth District)
416 Cannon House
Office Building
Washington, D.C. 20515
Phone: 202-225-4611
FAX: 202-226-0621

Rep. James T. Walsh (R)
(Twenty-Fifth District)
1330 Longworth House
Office Building
Washington, D.C. 20515
Phone: 202-225-3701
FAX: 202-225-4042

Rep. Maurice Hinchey (D)
(Twenty-Sixth District)
1313 Longworth House
Office Building
Washington, D.C. 20515
Phone: 202-225-6335
FAX: 202-226-0774

Rep. L. William Paxon (R)
(Twenty-Seventh District)
1314 Longworth House
Office Building
Washington, D.C. 20515
Phone: 202-225-5265
FAX: 202-225-5910

Rep. Louise M. Slaughter (D)
(Twenty-Eighth District)
2421 Rayburn House Office Building
Washington, D.C. 20515
Phone: 202-225-3615
FAX: 202-225-7822

Rep. John J. LaFalce (D)
(Twenty-Ninth District)
2310 Rayburn House
Office Building
Washington, D.C. 20515
Phone: 202-225-3231
FAX: 202-225-8693

Rep. Jack Quinn (R)
(Thirtieth District)
331 Cannon House
Office Building
Washington, D.C. 20515
Phone: 202-225-3306
FAX: 202-226-0347

Rep. Amory "Amo" Houghton, Jr. (R)
(Thirty-First District)
1110 Longworth House
Office Building
Washington, D.C. 20515
Phone: 202-225-3161
FAX: 202-225-5574

NORTH CAROLINA

Senators
Senator Jesse A. Helms (R)
403 Dirksen Senate
Office Building
Washington, D.C. 20510
Phone: 202-224-6342
FAX: 202-224-7588

Senator Lauch Faircloth (R)
702 Hart Senate
Office Building
Washington, D.C. 20510
Phone: 202-224-3154
FAX: 202-224-7406

Representatives
Rep. Eva Clayton (D)
(First District)
222 Cannon House
Office Building
Washington, D.C. 20515
Phone: 202-225-3101
FAX: 202-225-3354

Rep. David Funderburk (R)
(Second District)
2229 Rayburn House
Office Building
Washington, D.C. 20515
Phone: 202-225-4531
FAX: 202-225-1539

Rep. Walter Jones (R)
(Third District)
2436 Rayburn House
Office Building
Washington, D.C. 20515
Phone: 202-225-3415
FAX: 202-225-0666

Rep. Fred Heineman (D)
(Fourth District)
2458 Rayburn House
Office Building
Washington, D.C. 20515
Phone: 202-225-1784
FAX: 202-225-6314

Rep. Richard Burr (D)
(Fifth District)
2469 Rayburn House
Office Building
Washington, D.C. 20515
Phone: 202-225-2071
FAX: 202-225-4060

Rep. John Howard Coble (R)
(Sixth District)
403 Cannon House
Office Building
Washington, D.C. 20515
Phone: 202-225-3065
FAX: 202-225-8611

Rep. Charles G. Rose, III (D)
(Seventh District)
2230 Rayburn House
Office Building
Washington, D.C. 20515
Phone: 202-225-2731
FAX: 202-225-2470

Rep. W. G. "Bill" Hefner(D)
(Eighth District)
2470 Rayburn House
Office Building
Washington, D.C. 20515
Phone: 202-225-3715
FAX: 202-225-4036

Rep. Sue Myrick (R)
(Ninth District)
401 Cannon House
Office Building
Washington, D.C. 20515
Phone: 202-225-1976
FAX: 202-225-8995

Rep. T. Cass Ballenger (R)
(Tenth District)
2238 Rayburn House
Office Building
Washington, D.C. 20515
Phone: 202-225-2576
FAX: 202-225-0316

Rep. Charles H. Taylor (R)
(Eleventh District)
516 Cannon House
Office Building
Washington, D.C. 20515
Phone: 202-225-6401
FAX: 202-225-0519

Rep. Melvin Watt (D)
(Twelfth District)
1232 Longworth House
Office Building
Washington, D.C. 20515
Phone: 202-225-1510
FAX: 202-225-1512

NORTH DAKOTA

Senators
Senator Byron L. Dorgan (D)
713 Hart Senate
Office Building
Washington, D.C. 20510
Phone: 202-224-2551
FAX: 202-224-1193

Senator Kent Conrad (D)
724 Hart Senate
Office Building
Washington, D.C. 20510
Phone: 202-224-2043
FAX: 202-224-7776

Representative At Large
Rep. Earl Pomeroy (D)
318 Cannon House
Office Building
Washington, D.C. 20515
Phone: 202-225-2611
FAX: 202-226-0893

OHIO

Senators
Senator John H. Glenn, Jr. (D)
503 Hart Senate
Office Building
Washington, D.C. 20510
Phone: 202-224-3353
FAX: 202-224-7983

Senator Mike DeWine (R)
140 Russell Senate
Office Building
Washington, D.C. 20510
Phone: 202-224-2315
FAX: 202-224-6519

Representatives
Rep. Steve Chabot (D)
(First District)
503 Cannon House
Office Building
Washington, D.C. 20515
Phone: 202-225-2216
FAX: 202-225-4732

Rep. Rob Portman (R)
(Second District)
238 Cannon House
Office Building
Washington, D.C. 20515
Phone: 202-225-3164
FAX: 202-225-1992

Rep. Tony P. Hall (D)
(Third District)
2264 Rayburn House
Office Building
Washington, D.C. 20515
Phone: 202-225-6465
FAX: 202-225-6766

Rep. Michael G. Oxley (R)
(Fourth District)
2233 Rayburn House
Office Building
Washington, D.C. 20515
Phone: 202-225-2676
FAX: 202-226-1160

Rep. Paul E. Gillmor (R)
(Fifth District)
1203 Longworth House
Office Building
Washington, D.C. 20515
Phone: 202-225-6405
FAX: 202-225-1985

Rep. Frank Cremeans (R)
(Sixth District)
1429 Longworth House
Office Building
Washington, D.C. 20515
Phone: 202-225-5705
FAX: 202-226-0331

Rep. David L. Hobson (R)
(Seventh District)
1507 Longworth House
Office Building
Washington, D.C. 20515
Phone: 202-225-4324
FAX: 202-225-1984

Rep. John A. Boehner (R)
(Eighth District)
1020 Longworth House
Office Building
Washington, D.C. 20515
Phone: 202-225-6205
FAX: 202-225-0704

Rep. Marcy Kaptur (D)
(Ninth District)
2104 Rayburn House
Office Building
Washington, D.C. 20515
Phone: 202-225-4146
FAX: 202-225-7711

Rep. Martin R. Hoke (R)
(Tenth District)
212 Cannon House
Office Building
Washington, D.C. 20515
Phone: 202-225-5871
FAX: 202-226-0994

Rep. Louis Stokes (D)
(Eleventh District)
2365 Rayburn House
Office Building
Washington, D.C. 20515
Phone: 202-225-7032
FAX: 202-225-1339

Rep. John R. Kasich (R)
(Twelfth District)
1131 Longworth House
Office Building
Washington, D.C. 20515
Phone: 202-225-5355
FAX: (Unlisted)

Rep. Sherrod Brown (D)
(Thirteenth District)
1407 Longworth House
Office Building
Washington, D.C. 20515
Phone: 202-225-3401
FAX: 202-225-2266

Rep. Thomas C. Sawyer (D)
(Fourteenth District)
1414 Longworth House
Office Building
Washington, D.C. 20515
Phone: 202-225-5231
FAX: 202-225-5278

Rep. Deborah Pryce (R)
(Fifteenth District)
128 Cannon House
Office Building
Washington, D.C. 20515
Phone: 202-225-2015
FAX: 202-226-0986

Rep. Ralph S. Regula (R)
(Sixteenth District)
2309 Rayburn House
Office Building
Washington, D.C. 20515
Phone: 202-225-3876
FAX: 202-225-3059

Rep. James A. Traficant, Jr. (D)
(Seventeenth District)
2446 Rayburn House
Office Building
Washington, D.C. 20515
Phone: 202-225-5261
FAX: 202-225-3719

Rep. E. Bob Ney (R)
(Eighteenth District)
2183 Rayburn House
Office Building
Washington, D.C. 20515
Phone: 202-225-6265
FAX: 202-225-3087

Rep. Steven LaTourette (D)
(Nineteenth District)
431 Cannon House
Office Building
Washington, D.C. 20515
Phone: 202-225-5731
FAX: 202-225-9114

OKLAHOMA

Senators
Senator James Inhofe (R)
453 Russell Senate
Office Building
Washington, D.C. 20510
Phone: 202-224-4721
FAX: (Unlisted)

Senator Donald L. Nickles (R)
133 Hart Senate
Office Building
Washington, D.C. 20510
Phone: 202-224-5754
FAX: 202-224-6008

Representatives
Rep. Steve Largent (R)
(First District)
442 Cannon House
Office Building
Washington, D.C. 20515
Phone: 202-225-2211
FAX: 202-225-9187

Rep. Tom Coburn (R)
(Second District)
2329 Rayburn House
Office Building
Washington, D.C. 20515
Phone: 202-225-2701
FAX: 202-225-2796

Rep. William Brewster (D)
(Third District)
1727 Longworth House
Office Building
Washington, D.C. 20515
Phone: 202-225-4565
FAX: 202-225-9029

Rep. J. C. Watts (R)
(Fourth District)
2344 Rayburn House
Office Building
Washington, D.C. 20515
Phone: 202-225-6165
FAX: 202-225-9746

Rep. Earnest J. Istook (R)
(Fifth District)
1116 Longworth House
Office Building
Washington, D.C. 20515
Phone: 202-225-2132
FAX: 202-226-1463

Rep. Frank Lucas (R)
(Sixth District)
2206 Rayburn House
Office Building
Washington, D.C. 20515
Phone: 202-225-5565
FAX: 202-225-8698

OREGON

Senators
Senator Mark O. Hatfield (R)
711 Hart Senate
Office Building
Washington, D.C. 20510
Phone: 202-224-3753
FAX: 202-224-0276

Senator Robert William Packwood (R)
259 Russell Senate
Office Building
Washington, D.C. 20510
Phone: 202-224-5244
FAX: 202-228-3576

Representatives
Rep. Elizabeth Furse (D)
(First District)
316 Cannon House
Office Building
Washington, D.C. 20515
Phone: 202-225-0855
FAX: 202-225-9497

Rep. Wes Cooley (R)
(Second District)
118 Cannon House
Office Building
Washington, D.C. 20515
Phone: 202-225-6730
FAX: 202-225-3129

Rep. Ron Wyden (D)
(Third District)
1111 Longworth House
Office Building
Washington, D.C. 20515
Phone: 202-225-4811
FAX: 202-225-8941

Rep. Peter A. DeFazio (D)
(Fourth District)
1233 Longworth House
Office Building
Washington, D.C. 20515
Phone: 202-225-6416
FAX: 202-225-0694

Rep. Catherine Webber (D)
(Fifth District)
218 Cannon House
Office Building
Washington, D.C. 20510
Phone: 202-225-5711
FAX: 202-225-9477

PENNSYLVANIA

Senators
Senator Rick Santorum (R)
521 Dirksen Senate
Office Building
Washington, D.C. 20510
Phone: 202-224-6324
FAX: 202-224-4161

Senator Arlen Specter (R)
530 Hart Senate
Office Building
Washington, D.C. 20510
Phone: 202-224-4254
FAX: 202-224-1893

Representatives
Rep. Thomas M. Foglietta (D)
(First District)
341 Cannon House
Office Building
Washington, D.C. 20515
Phone: 202-225-4731
FAX: 202-225-0088

Rep. Chaka Fattah (D)
(Second District)
410 Cannon House
Office Building
Washington, D.C. 20515
Phone: 202-225-4001
FAX: 202-225-7362

Rep. Robert A. Borski (D)
(Third District)
2161 Rayburn House
Office Building
Washington, D.C. 20515
Phone: 202-225-8251
FAX: 202-225-4628

Rep. Ron Klink (D)
(Fourth District)
1130 Longworth House
Office Building
Washington, D.C. 20515
Phone: 202-225-2565
FAX: 202-226-2274

Rep. William F. Clinger, Jr. (R)
(Fifth District)
2160 Rayburn House
Office Building
Washington, D.C. 20515
Phone: 202-225-5121
FAX: 202-225-4681

Rep. Tim Holden (D)
(Sixth District)
1421 Longworth House
Office Building
Washington, D.C. 20515
Phone: 202-225-5546
FAX: 202-226-0996

Rep. Wayne C. Weldon (R)
(Seventh District)
2452 Cannon House
Office Building
Washington, D.C. 20515
Phone: 202-225-2011
FAX: 202-225-8137

Rep. Jim Greenwood (R)
(Eighth District)
515 Cannon House
Office Building
Washington, D.C. 20515
Phone: 202-225-4276
FAX: 202-225-9511

Rep. E. G. "Bud" Shuster (R)
(Ninth District)
2188 Rayburn House
Office Building
Washington, D.C. 20515
Phone: 202-225-2431
FAX: 202-225-2486

Rep. Joseph M. McDade (R)
(Tenth District)
2370 Rayburn House
Office Building
Washington, D.C. 20515
Phone: 202-225-3731
FAX: 202-225-9594

Rep. Paul E. Kanjorski (D)
(Eleventh District)
2429 Cannon House
Office Building
Washington, D.C. 20515
Phone: 202-225-6511
FAX: 202-225-9024

Rep. John P. Murtha (D)
(Twelfth District)
2423 Rayburn House
Office Building
Washington, D.C. 20515
Phone: 202-225-2065
FAX: 202-225-5709

Rep. Jon Fox (R)
(Thirteenth District)
1516 Rayburn House
Office Building
Washington, D.C. 20515
Phone: 202-225-6111
FAX: 202-226-0798

Rep. William J. Coyne (D)
(Fourteenth District)
2455 Rayburn House
Office Building
Washington, D.C. 20515
Phone: 202-225-2301
FAX: 202-225-1844

Rep. Paul McHale (D)
(Fifteenth District)
511 Rayburn House
Office Building
Washington, D.C. 20515
Phone: 202-225-6411
FAX: 202-225-5320

Rep. Robert S. Walker (R)
(Sixteenth District)
2369 Rayburn House
Office Building
Washington, D.C. 20515
Phone: 202-225-2411
FAX: 202-225-2484

Rep. George W. Gekas (R)
(Seventeenth District)
2410 Longworth House
Office Building
Washington, D.C. 20515
Phone: 202-225-4315
FAX: 202-225-8440

Rep. Michael Doyle (D)
(Eighteenth District)
1222 Longworth House
Office Building
Washington, D.C. 20515
Phone: 202-225-2135
FAX: 202-225-7747

Rep. William F. Goodling (R)
(Nineteenth District)
2263 Rayburn House
Office Building
Washington, D.C. 20515
Phone: 202-225-5836
FAX: 202-226-1000

Rep. Frank Mascara (D)
(Twentieth District)
2210 Rayburn House
Office Building
Washington, D.C. 20515
Phone: 202-225-4665
FAX: 202-225-4772

Rep. Philip English (R)
(Twenty-First District)
1714 Longworth House
Office Building
Washington, D.C. 20515
Phone: 202-225-5406
FAX: 202-225-1081

RHODE ISLAND

Senators
Senator Claiborne Pell (D)
335 Russell Senate
Office Building
Washington, D.C. 20510
Phone: 202-224-4642
FAX: 202-224-4680

Senator John H. Chafee (R)
567 Dirksen Senate
Office Building
Washington, D.C. 20510
Phone: 202-224-2921
FAX: 202-224-7472

Representatives
Rep. Patrick Kennedy (D)
(First District)
326 Cannon House
Office Building
Washington, D.C. 20515
Phone: 202-225-4911
FAX: 202-225-4417

Rep. John F. Reed (R)
(Second District)
1510 Longworth House
Office Building
Washington, D.C. 20515
Phone: 202-225-2735
FAX: 202-225-9580

SOUTH CAROLINA

Senators
Senator James Strom Thurmond (R)
217 Russell Senate
Office Building
Washington, D.C. 20510
Phone: 202-224-5972
FAX: 202-224-1300

Senator Ernest F. Hollings (D)
125 Russell Senate
Office Building
Washington, D.C. 20510
Phone: 202-224-6121
FAX: 202-224-3573

Representatives
Rep. Mark Sanford (R)
(First District)
231 Cannon House
Office Building
Washington, D.C. 20515
Phone: 202-225-3176
FAX: 202-225-4340

Rep. Floyd D. Spence (R)
(Second District)
2405 Rayburn House
Office Building
Washington, D.C. 20515
Phone: 202-225-2452
FAX: 202-225-2455

Rep. Lindsey Graham (R)
(Third District)
221 Cannon House
Office Building
Washington, D.C. 20515
Phone: 202-225-5301
FAX: 202-225-5383

Rep. Bob Inglis (R)
(Fourth District)
1237 Longworth House
Office Building
Washington, D.C. 20515
Phone: 202-225-6030
FAX: 202-226-1177

Rep. John M. Spratt, Jr. (D)
(Fifth District)
1536 Longworth House
Office Building
Washington, D.C. 20515
Phone: 202-225-5501
FAX: 202-225-0464

Rep. James E. Clyburn (D)
(Sixth District)
319 Cannon House
Office Building
Washington, D.C. 20515
Phone: 202-225-3315
FAX: 202-225-2313

SOUTH DAKOTA

Senators
Senator Larry Pressler (R)
283 Rayburn House
Office Building
Washington, D.C. 20510
Phone: 202-224-5842
FAX: 202-224-1630

Senator Thomas Andrew Daschle (D)
317 Hart Senate
Office Building
Washington, D.C. 20510
Phone: 202-224-2321
FAX: 202-224-2047

Representative At Large
Rep. Timothy P. Johnson (D)
2438 Rayburn House
Office Building
Washington, D.C. 20515
Phone: 202-225-2801
FAX: 202-225-2427

TENNESSEE

Senators
Senator Fred Thompson (R)
363 Russell Senate
Office Building
Washington, D.C. 20510
Phone: 202-224-3344
FAX: 202-224-8062

Senator Bill Frist (R)
506 Dirksen Senate
Office Building
Washington, D.C. 20510
Phone: 202-224-1036
FAX: 202-228-3679

Representatives
Rep. James H. Quillen (R)
(First District)
102 Cannon House
Office Building
Washington, D.C. 20515
Phone: 202-225-6356
FAX: 202-225-7812

Rep. John J. Duncan, Jr. (R)
(Second District)
115 Cannon House
Office Building
Washington, D.C. 20515
Phone: 202-225-5435
FAX: 202-225-6440

Rep. Zach Wamp (R)
(Third District)
2406 Rayburn House
Office Building
Washington, D.C. 20515
Phone: 202-225-3271
FAX: 202-225-6974

Rep. Van Hilleary (R)
(Fourth District)
125 Cannon House
Office Building
Washington, D.C. 20515
Phone: 202-225-6831
FAX: 202-225-4520

Rep. Bob Clement (D)
(Fifth District)
1230 Cannon House
Office Building
Washington, D.C. 20515
Phone: 202-225-4311
FAX: 202-226-1035

Rep. Barton J. Gordon (D)
(Sixth District)
103 Cannon House
Office Building
Washington, D.C. 20515
Phone: 202-225-4231
FAX: 202-225-6887

Rep. Ed Bryant (R)
(Seventh District)
339 Cannon House
Office Building
Washington, D.C. 20515
Phone: 202-225-2811
FAX: 202-225-2814

Rep. John S. Tanner (D)
(Eighth District)
1427 Longworth House
Office Building
Washington, D.C. 20515
Phone: 202-225-4714
FAX: 202-225-1765

Rep. Harold Eugene Ford (D)
(Ninth District)
2211 Rayburn House
Office Building
Washington, D.C. 20515
Phone: 202-225-3265
FAX: 202-225-9215

TEXAS

Senators
Senator Phil Gramm (R)
370 Russell Senate
Office Building
Washington, D.C. 20510
Phone: 202-224-2934
FAX: 202-228-2856

Senator Kathryn "Kay" Bailey Hutchison (R)
703 Hart Senate Office Building
Washington, D.C. 20510
Phone: 202-224-5922
FAX: 202-224-0776

Representatives
Rep. Jim Chapman (D)
(First District)
2417 Rayburn House
Office Building
Washington, D.C. 20515
Phone: 202-225-3035
FAX: 202-225-7265

Rep. Charles N. Wilson (D)
(Second District)
2256 Rayburn House
Office Building
Washington, D.C. 20515
Phone: 202-225-2401
FAX: 202-225-1764

Rep. Sam Johnson (R)
(Third District)
1030 Longworth House
Office Building
Washington, D.C. 20515
Phone: 202-225-4201
FAX: 202-225-1485

Rep. Ralph M. Hall (D)
(Fourth District)
2236 Rayburn House
Office Building
Washington, D.C. 20515
Phone: 202-225-6673
FAX: 202-225-3332

Rep. John Wiley Bryant (D)
(Fifth District)
205 Cannon House
Office Building
Washington, D.C. 20515
Phone: 202-225-2231
FAX: 202-225-9721

Rep. Joe Linus Barton (R)
(Sixth District)
1514 Longworth House
Office Building
Washington, D.C. 20515
Phone: 202-225-2002
FAX: 202-225-3052

Rep. Bill Archer (R)
(Seventh District)
1236 Longworth House
Office Building
Washington, D.C. 20515
Phone: 202-225-2571
FAX: 202-225-4381

Rep. Jack Fields (R)
(Eighth District)
2228 Rayburn House
Office Building
Washington, D.C. 20515
Phone: 202-225-4901
FAX: 202-225-2772

Rep. Steve Stockman (R)
(Ninth District)
2449 Rayburn Hous
Office Building
Washington, D.C. 20515
Phone: 202-225-6565
FAX: 202-225-1584

Rep. Lloyd Doggett (D)
(Tenth District)
242 Cannon House
Office Building
Washington, D.C. 20515
Phone: 202-225-4865
FAX: 202-225-3018

Rep. Chet Edwards (D)
(Eleventh District)
328 Cannon House
Office Building
Washington, D.C. 20515
Phone: 202-225-6105
FAX: 202-225-0350

Rep. Preston M. "Pete" Geren (D)
(Twelfth District)
1730 Longworth House
Office Building
Washington, D.C. 20515
Phone: 202-225-5071
FAX: 202-225-2786

Rep. William Thornberry (R)
(Thirteenth District)
126 Cannon House
Office Building
Washington, D.C. 20515
Phone: 202-225-3706
FAX: 202-225-6142

Rep. Greg Laughlin (R)
(Fourteenth District)
236 Cannon House
Office Building
Washington, D.C. 20515
Phone: 202-225-2831
FAX: 202-225-1108

Rep. E. "Kika" de la Garza (D)
(Fifteenth District)
1401 Longworth House
Office Building
Washington, D.C. 20515
Phone: 202-225-2531
FAX: 202-225-2534

Rep. Ronald D'Emory Coleman (D)
(Sixteenth District)
440 Cannon House
Office Building
Washington, D.C. 20515
Phone: 202-225-4831
FAX: 202-225-4831

Rep. Charles W. Stenholm (D)
(Seventeenth District)
1211 Longworth House
Office Building
Washington, D.C. 20515
Phone: 202-225-6605
FAX: 202-225-2234

Rep. Shelia Lee (D)
(Eighteenth District)
1711 Longworth House
Office Building
Washington, D.C. 20515
Phone: 202-225-3816
FAX: 202-225-6186

Rep. Larry Ed Combest (R)
(Nineteenth District)
1511 Longworth House
Office Building
Washington, D.C. 20515
Phone: 202-225-4005
FAX: 202-225-9615

Rep. Henry B. Gonzalez (D)
(Twentieth District)
2413 Rayburn House
Office Building
Washington, D.C. 20515
Phone: 202-225-3236
FAX: 202-225-1915

Rep. Lamar S. Smith (R)
(Twenty-First District)
2443 Rayburn House
Office Building
Washington, D.C. 20515
Phone: 202-225-4236
FAX: 202-225-8628

Rep. Tom DeLay (R)
(Twenty-Second District)
407 Cannon House
Office Building
Washington, D.C. 20515
Phone: 202-225-5951
FAX: 202-225-5241

Rep. Henry Bonilla (R)
(Twenty-Third District)
1529 Longworth House
Office Building
Washington, D.C. 20515
Phone: 202-225-4511
FAX: 202-225-2237

Rep. Martin Frost (D)
(Twenty-Fourth District)
2459 Rayburn House
Office Building
Washington, D.C. 20515
Phone: 202-225-3605
FAX: 202-225-4951

Rep. Ken Bentsen (D)
(Twenty-Fifth District)
303 Cannon House
Office Building
Washington, D.C. 20515
Phone: 202-225-7508
FAX: 202-225-4210

Rep. Richard K. Armey (R)
(Twenty-Sixth District)
301 Cannon House
Office Building
Washington, D.C. 20515
Phone: 202-225-7772
FAX: 202-225-7614

Rep. Solomon P. Ortiz (D)
(Twenty-Seventh District)
2136 Rayburn House
Office Building
Washington, D.C. 20515
Phone: 202-225-7742
FAX: 202-226-1134

Rep. Frank Tejeda (D)
(Twenty-Eighth District)
323 Cannon House
Office Building
Washington, D.C. 20515
Phone: 202-225-1640
FAX: 202-225-1641

Rep. Gene Green (D)
(Twenty-Ninth District)
1004 Longworth House
Office Building
Washington, D.C. 20515
Phone: 202-225-1688
FAX: 202-225-9903

Rep. Eddie B. Johnson (D)
(Thirtieth District)
1721 Longworth House
Office Building
Washington, D.C. 20515
Phone: 202-225-8885
FAX: 202-226-1477

UTAH

Senators
Senator Robert Bennett (R)
241 Dirksen Senate
Office Building
Washington, D.C. 20510
Phone: 202-224-5444
FAX: 202-224-6717

Senator Orrin G. Hatch (R)
135 Russell Senate
Office Building
Washington, D.C. 20510
Phone: 202-224-5251
FAX: 202-224-6331

Representatives
Rep. James V. Hansen (R)
(First District)
2466 Rayburn House
Office Building
Washington, D.C. 20515
Phone: 202-225-0453
FAX: 202-225-5857

Rep. Karen Shepherd (D)
(Second District)
414 Cannon House
Office Building
Washington, D.C. 20515
Phone: 202-225-3011
FAX: 202-226-0354

Rep. William Orton (D)
(Third District)
1122 Longworth House
Office Building
Washington, D.C. 20515
Phone: 202-225-7751
FAX: 202-226-1223

VERMONT

Senators
Senator Patrick Leahy (D)
433 Russell Senate
Office Building
Washington, D.C. 20510
Phone: 202-224-4242
FAX: 202-224-3595

Senator James M. Jeffords (R)
513 Hart Senate
Office Building
Washington, D.C. 20510
Phone: 202-224-5141
FAX: 202-224-8330

Representative At Large
Rep. Bernard Sanders (Soc)
213 Cannon House
Office Building
Washington, D.C. 20515
Phone: 202-225-4115
FAX: 202-225-6790

VIRGINIA

Senators
Senator John W. Warner (R)
225 Russell Senate
Office Building
Washington, D.C. 20510
Phone: 202-224-2023
FAX: 202-224-6295

Senator Charles S. Robb (D)
493 Russell Senate
Office Building
Washington, D.C. 20510
Phone: 202-224-4024
FAX: 202-224-8689

Representatives
Rep. Herbert H. Bateman (R)
(First District)
2350 Rayburn House
Office Building
Washington, D.C. 20515
Phone: 202-225-4261
FAX: 202-225-4382

Rep. Owen B. Pickett (D)
(Second District)
2430 Rayburn House
Office Building
Washington, D.C. 20515
Phone: 202-225-4215
FAX: 202-225-4218

Rep. Robert C. Scott (D)
(Third District)
501 Cannon House
Office Building
Washington, D.C. 20515
Phone: 202-225-8351
FAX: 202-225-8354

Rep. Norman Sisisky (D)
(Fourth District)
2352 Cannon House
Office Building
Washington, D.C. 20515
Phone: 202-225-6365
FAX: 202-226-1170

Rep. Lewis F. Payne, Jr. (D)
(Fifth District)
1119 Longworth House
Office Building
Washington, D.C. 20515
Phone: 202-225-4711
FAX: 202-226-1147

Rep. Robert W. Goodlatte (R)
(Sixth District)
214 Cannon House
Office Building
Washington, D.C. 20515
Phone: 202-225-5431
FAX: 202-225-9681

Rep. Thomas J. Bliley, Jr. (R)
(Seventh District)
2241 Rayburn House
Office Building
Washington, D.C. 20515
Phone: 202-225-2815
FAX: 202-225-0011

Rep. James P. Moran, Jr. (D)
(Eighth District)
430 Cannon House
Office Building
Washington, D.C. 20515
Phone: 202-225-4376
FAX: 202-225-0017

Rep. Rick Boucher (D)
(Ninth District)
2245 Rayburn House
Office Building
Washington, D.C. 20515
Phone: 202-225-3861
FAX: 202-225-0442

Rep. Frank R. Wolf (R)
(Tenth District)
104 Cannon House
Office Building
Washington, D.C. 20515
Phone: 202-225-5136
FAX: 202-225-0437

Rep. Thomas Davis (R)
(Eleventh District)
1609 Longworth House
Office Building
Washington, D.C. 20515
Phone: 202-225-1492
FAX: 202-225-2274

WASHINGTON

Senators
Senator Patty Murray (D)
302 Hart Senate
Office Building
Washington, D.C. 20510
Phone: 202-224-2621
FAX: 202-224-0238

Senator Slade Gorton (R)
730 Hart Senate
Office Building
Washington, D.C. 20510
Phone: 202-224-3441
FAX: 202-224-9393

Representatives
Rep. Rick White (R)
(First District)
1520 Longworth House
Office Building
Washington, D.C. 20515
Phone: 202-225-6311
FAX: 202-225-2286

Rep. Jack Metcalf (R)
(Second District)
1502 Longworth House
Office Building
Washington, D.C. 20515
Phone: 202-225-2605
FAX: 202-225-2608

Rep. Linda Smith (R)
(Third District)
1527 Longworth House
Office Building
Washington, D.C. 20515
Phone: 202-225-3536
FAX: 202-225-9095

Rep. Doc Hastings (R)
(Fourth District)
1431 Longworth House
Office Building
Washington, D.C. 20515
Phone: 202-225-5816
FAX: 202-226-1137

Rep. George Nethercutt (R)
(Fifth District)
1201 Longworth House
Office Building
Washington, D.C. 20515
Phone: 202-225-2006
FAX: 202-225-7181

Rep. Norman D. Dicks (D)
(Sixth District)
2467 Rayburn House
Office Building
Washington, D.C. 20515
Phone: 202-225-5916
FAX: 202-226-1176

Rep. James A. McDermott (D)
(Seventh District)
1707 Longworth House
Office Building
Washington, D.C. 20515
Phone: 202-225-3106
FAX: 202-225-9212

Rep. Jennifer Dunn (R)
(Eighth District)
1641 Longworth House
Office Building
Washington, D.C. 20515
Phone: 202-225-7761
FAX: 202-225-8673

Rep. Randy Tate (R)
(Ninth District)
1535 Longworth House
Office Building
Washington, D.C. 20515
Phone: 202-225-8901
FAX: 202-226-2361

WEST VIRGINIA

Senators
Senator Robert C. Byrd (D)
311 Hart Senate Office Building
Washington, D.C. 20510
Phone: 202-224-3954
FAX: 202-224-4025

Senator John D. Rockefeller, IV (D)
109 Hart Senate Office Building
Washington, D.C. 20510
Phone: 202-224-6472
FAX: 202-224-7665

Representatives
Rep. Alan B. Mollohan (D)
(First District)
2242 Rayburn House
Office Building
Washington, D.C. 20515
Phone: 202-225-4172
FAX: 202-225-7564

Rep. Robert W. Wise (D)
(Second District)
2434 Rayburn House
Office Building
Washington, D.C. 20515
Phone: 202-225-2711
FAX: 202-225-7856

Rep. Nick Joe Rahall, II (D)
(Third District)
2269 Rayburn House
Office Building
Washington, D.C. 20515
Phone: 202-225-3452
FAX: 202-225-9061

WISCONSIN

Senators
Senator Russell Feingold (D)
502 Hart Senate
Office Building
Washington, D.C. 20510
Phone: 202-224-5323
FAX: 202-224-2725

Senator Herb Kohl (D)
330 Hart Senate
Office Building
Washington, D.C. 20510
Phone: 202-224-5653
FAX: 202-224-9787

Representatives
Rep. Mark Neumann (R)
(First District)
1719 Longworth House
Office Building
Washington, D.C. 20515
Phone: 202-225-3031
FAX: 202-225-9820

Rep. Scott L. Klug (R)
(Second District)
1224 Longworth House
Office Building
Washington, D.C. 20515
Phone: 202-225-2906
FAX: 202-225-6942

Rep. Steven C. Gunderson (R)
(Third District)
2235 Rayburn House
Office Building
Washington, D.C. 20515
Phone: 202-225-5506
FAX: 202-225-6195

Rep. Gerald D. Kleczka (D)
(Fourth District)
2301 Rayburn House
Office Building
Washington, D.C. 20515
Phone: 202-225-4572
FAX: 202-225-0719

Rep. Thomas M. Barrett (D)
(Fifth District)
313 Cannon House
Office Building
Washington, D.C. 20515
Phone: 202-225-3571
FAX: 202-225-2185

Rep. Thomas E. Petri (R)
(Sixth District)
2262 Rayburn House
Office Building
Washington, D.C. 20515
Phone: 202-225-2476
FAX: 202-225-2356

Rep. David R. Obey (D)
(Seventh District)
2462 Rayburn House
Office Building
Washington, D.C. 20515
Phone: 202-225-3365
FAX: 202-225-0561

Rep. Toby Roth (R)
(Eighth District)
2234 Rayburn House
Office Building
Washington, D.C. 20515
Phone: 202-225-5665
FAX: 202-225-0087

Rep. E. James Sensenbrenner, Jr. (R)
(Ninth District)
2332 Rayburn House
Office Building
Washington, D.C. 20515
Phone: 202-225-5101
FAX: 202-225-3190

WYOMING

Senators
Senator Craig Thomas (R)
237 Russell Senate
Office Building
Washington, D.C. 20510
Phone: 202-224-6441
FAX: 202-224-3230

Senator Alan K. Simpson (R)
261 Dirksen Senate
Office Building
Washington, D.C. 20510
Phone: 202-224-3424
FAX: 202-224-1315

Representative At Large
Rep. Barbara Cubin (R)
1019 Longworth
House Office Building
Washington, D.C. 20505
Phone: 202-225-2311
FAX: 202-225-0726

Bibliography

Adler, T. and R. Cowen. "Proposed Federal Budget Keeps R&D Afloat." *Science News*. February 12, 1994.

Amos, Orley M., Jr., *Economic Literacy*. Career Press, Hawthorne, N.J., 1994.

Bagby, Wesley M. *Introduction to Social Science and Contemporary Issues*. Nelson-Hall, Chicago, 1995.

Baumol, William J. and Alan S. Blinder. *Economics Principles and Policy*. Harcourt Brace Jovanovich, San Diego, 1991.

Bernstein, Aaron. "Inequality." *Business Week*. August 15, 1994.

"Best Annual Reports." *Chief Executive Officer*. October 1992.

Biggs, Barton M. and Byron R. Wien. *Economics: The Rebound After the Pause*. Morgan Stanley & Co. Incorporated. June 28, 1995.

Black, Gordon S. and Benjamin D. *The Politics of American Discontent*. John Wiley & Sons, New York, 1994.

Calleo, David. *The Bankrupting of America*. Avon Books, New York, 1992.

Cane, Michael Allan. *Guide to Federal Income Taxes*. Dell, New York, 1995.

Caplan, Richard and John Fetter. *State of the Union 1994*. Westview Press, Boulder, Col., 1994.

Cato Handbook for Congress, The. Cato Institute, Washington, 1995.

Caves, Richard E., Jeffery A. Frankel and Ronald W. Jones. *World Trade and Payments*. HarperCollins, New York, 1993.

Collins, James C. and Jerry I. Porras. *Built to Last*. HarperBusiness, New York, 1994.

Contract with America. Random House, New York, 1994.

Economic Report of the President 1995, 1994, 1993. National Council of Economic Advisors: Transmitted to the Congress of the United States.

Eisner, Robert. *The Misunderstood Economy: What Counts and How to Count It*. Harvard Business School Press, Cambridge, Mass., 1994.

Executive Summary Fiscal Year 1996 Budget. Department of Housing and Urban Development.

"Facts on Social Security: The Old Age and Survivors Trust Fund." National Academy on Aging. June 1995.

Feldstein, Martin. *American Economic Policy in the 1980s*. National Bureau of Economic Research, Cambridge, Mass., 1994.

Feldstein, Martin. *The Risk of Economic Crisis*. University of Chicago Press, Chicago, 1991.

Figgie, Harry E. *Bankruptcy 1995*. Little, Brown and Company, Boston, 1992.

Fuchs, Lawrence H. *The American Kaleidoscope*. University Press of New England, Hanover, N.H., 1990.

Gaebler, Ted and David Osborne. *Reinventing Government*. Penguin, New York, 1993.

Galbraith, John Kenneth. *Whence It Came, Where It Went*. Houghton Mifflin Company, Boston, 1995.

Heilbroner, Robert and Lester Thurow. *Economics Explained*. Simon & Schuster, New York, 1994.

Howard, Philip K. *The Death of Common Sense*. Random House, New York, 1994.

"HUD Reinvention from Blueprint to Action." U.S. Department of Housing and Urban Development. March 1995.

Information Please Almanac 1995, 1994. Houghton Mifflin, Boston, 1994.

Kaplan, Martin and Naomi Weiss. *What the IRS Doesn't Want You to Know*. Villard Books, New York, 1994.

Kennedy, Paul. *Preparing for the Twenty-First Century*. Random House, New York, 1993.

Krugman, Paul. *Peddling Prosperity*. W. W. Norton & Company, New York, 1994.

Krugman, Paul R. and Maurice Obstfeld. *International Economics*. HarperCollins, New York, 1991.

Kuttner, Robert. "The Big Snag in the Global Economy." *Business Week*. August 1, 1994.

Mankiw, Gregory N. *Macroeconomics*. Worth Publishers, New York, 1992.

Marshall, Will and Martin Schram. *Mandate for Change*. Berkley Books, New York, 1993.

"Medicare Watch." *AARP Bulletin*. July-August, 1995.

Moore, Stephen. *Government: America's Number One Growth Industry*. Institute for Policy Innovation, Texas, 1995.

Moore, Stephen, ed. *Restoring the Dream*. Times Books, New York, 1995.

Morgan, Iwan W. *Deficit Government*. Ivan R. Dee, Chicago, 1995.

"New Economy: A Special Report." *Fortune*. June 27, 1994.

"New Tax Law." *Ernst and Young*. John Wiley & Sons, New York, 1993.

"1995 Guide to Health Insurance for People with Medicare." National Association of Insurance Commissioners and the Health Care Financing Administration of the U.S. Department of Health and Human Services. 1995.

Nixon, Richard. *Beyond Peace*. Random House, New York, 1994.

Perot, Ross. *Medicare*. Hyperion, New York, 1994.

Perot, Ross with Pat Choate. *Save Your Job, Save Our Country*. Hyperion, New York, 1993.

Phillips, Kevin. *The Politics of the Rich and Poor*. HarperCollins, New York, 1989.

Pindyck, Robert S. and Daniel L. Rubinfeld. *Microeconomics*. Macmillan, New York, 1992.

Reich, Robert B. *The Work of Nations*. Alfred A. Knopf, New York, 1991.

Rosen, Harvey S. *Public Finance*. Irwin, Chicago, 1995.

Sachs, Jeffrey D. and Felipe Larrain B. *Macroeconomics in the Global Economy*. Prentice Hall, Englewood Cliffs, N.J., 1993.

Schlesinger, Arthur M. *The Disuniting of America*. W. W. Norton & Company, New York, 1992.

"Social Security: Brief History of the Social Security Administration." Social Security Administration. March 31, 1995.

"Social Security: Understanding Social Security." Social Security Administration. April 1995.

Statistical Abstract of the United States 1994. Washington, 1994.

Thurow, Lester. *Head to Head*. Time Warner, New York, 1993.

"Treasury Bulletin: International Statistics." U.S. Treasury Department. June 1995.

"Treasury Department: Consolidated Statement of Financial Position. Fiscal Year 1993, 1994." U.S. Treasury Department. September 30, 1993–1994.

Weinberger, Casper. "A Domestic Foreign Policy." *Forbes*. July 4, 1994.

"Will You Be Able to Retire?" *Fortune*. September 11, 1995.

Who's Who in Congress, 1995. 104th Congress, Congressional Quarterly, Inc., 1995.

World Almanac and Book of Facts 1995. Funk & Wagnalls, Mahwah, N.J., 1995.

World Almanac of U.S. Politics, 1993–1995. Funk & Wagnalls, Mahwah, N.J., 1993.

Your Medicare Handbook 1995. Health Care Financing Administration. 1995.